LEAVE THE GHOST LIGHT BURNING

ILLUMINATING FALLBACK IN EMBRACE OF THE FULLNESS OF YOU

VALERIE LIVESAY

KAIROS

PUBLISHING

SAN MARCOS, CALIFORNIA

Kairos Publishing
San Marcos, California

© 2022 Valerie Livesay
All rights reserved.

No part of this book may be reproduced or transmitted in any form or by any means, electronic or mechanical, including photocopying and recording without the prior written permission of Kairos Publishing. For permissions contact: inquiries@kairospublishing.net. Reviewers may quote brief passages in reviews.

ISBN 979-8-9869399-0-2 (paper)
ISBN 979-8-9869399-1-9 (ebook)

Library of Congress Control Number: 2022918213

Cover illustration: © Rachel Phillips, 2022
"Backstage" from the series Ghost Light Theaters.

Cover design by Tea Filipi
Editing by Erica Ellis

Visit the author's website at www.ghostlightleadership.com.

To Townsend and Sloane who see and love the fullness of me. It is my hope that in so doing you may be better able to see and love the fullness of your beautifully imperfect selves.

To Sonnie who has sat by my side in the depths of the pit of fallback more times than I can count, and whose accompaniment, acceptance, and love for me in my smallness, in my bigness, and all of the places in between offer me the courage to climb back into the illumination of the ghost light.

To Stephanie, my bright star. Your voice dances on the wind, recollecting the me who was, who is, who is becoming…still.

CONTENTS

Foreword by Jennifer Garvey Berger vii
Introduction 1
Chapter 1.
The Fluidity of Development 5
Chapter 2.
What Is Fallback? 12
Chapter 3.
Prologue - Meet Diego, Robbin, and Octavia 18
Chapter 4.
Ghost Light 29
Chapter 5.
Noticing 32
Chapter 6.
Valerie - Noticing 40
Chapter 7.
Your Turn to Notice 43
Chapter 8.
Reflecting 45
Chapter 9.
Diego - Reflecting 52
Chapter 10.
Your Turn to Reflect 63
Chapter 11.
Recognizing Triggers 65
Chapter 12.
Robbin - Recognizing Triggers 75
Chapter 13.
Your Turn to Recognize Triggers 91
Chapter 14.
Recovering and Growing 93
Chapter 15.
Octavia - Recovering and Growing 105
Chapter 16.
Your Turn to Recover and Grow 123
Chapter 17.
Epilogue 126
Chapter 18.
Leaving the Ghost Light Burning for Others 138
Chapter 19.
Conclusion - Illuminating the Fullness of You 149

Afterword - Still Fencing the Field of Fallback 153
Grateful Fors 165
Notes 171
Selected Bibliography 179
About the Author 181

FOREWORD
BY JENNIFER GARVEY BERGER

You know this feeling. You have had a bad day, a bad week. You're as brittle as a crystal goblet and as likely to shatter. And then one more thing piles on, and you become your reactions: your lips move without your bidding, yelling or crying or whatever your lips do when you can't restrain them. You lash out loudly, or hear your voice go cold, or curl up into a small silent ball. One tiny piece of you might mutter that you are being unfair, a little outrageous, but that voice is overcome by the righteous coursing anger or the electric anxiety or the profound sadness that washes over you like a rogue wave.

And then, in an hour or a week or a month, it passes, and you find yourself again. And when you look back on that you that you were, it sounds something like:

"I was just not myself."

"I was acting like a two-year-old!"

"I lost it yesterday!"

And, in one of my favourite expressions, "I threw all my toys out of the pram."

This sense—that we are young, that we are out of control, that we are lost—is familiar to us. This is the weather pattern of "fallback." When the storm passes, we find ourselves wet and muddy on the shore, maybe ashamed of ourselves or maybe defensive and blaming. We vow that won't happen again—it is unpleasant whether it's our fault or the fault of whatever pushed us over the edge. We beat ourselves up or feel trapped and horrible in whatever context we were in when we lost ourselves: our work, our marriage, our family. In this book, Dr. Valerie Livesay invites us to look underneath those one-liners, beneath the blame, beneath the shame, and make sense of what's going on, make friends with those parts that feel two years old. She invites us to find ourselves even when we are most lost.

This is no effortless inquiry, though, no Five Steps to Ensuring You're Never Unhappy Again. Instead, this book should come with a warning stamp on the front cover: *BEWARE! Monsters lurking inside.* And they might be the most dangerous monsters you have ever known because they are not outside you but inside your skin, whispering in your ear right now. And here is the bad news: you cannot escape. Val is going to make it impossible for you to believe those monsters in your head will ever go away. In fact, she's going to encourage you to set a lovely table for them, pour out cups of tea, and get to know one another.

You might think that perhaps today isn't a good day for tea with your inner monster. The world is too tough right now, too filled with scary monsters outside us: pandemics, climate change, authoritarian leaders. You would be forgiven for imagining there is no good day to break bread with any inner monsters if you can avoid it. And you've been avoiding it for years.

But Val taught me nearly a decade ago that we avoid the inner monsters at our peril. I had been a developmentalist more than a dozen years when I met Val. Before Val, I had reached out a (sometimes reluctant) hand of empathy to those smaller parts of us that lie in wait for our exhaustion or rage or overwhelm. I had acknowledged them and tried to make space for them in both my theories and in my sense of myself. But I absolutely didn't want to get to know them, and, if I'm honest, I sort of hoped I would someday be able to sneak away from them and leave them behind, like slipping out the restaurant's back door without paying the bill.

Over the years I have worked with Val, though, I've discovered that when I try to sneak away, these monsters chase after me. They claw and rage and scare away little children. This happens to you too. It happens to us all, no matter how much we try to prevent it from happening or deny it when it does.

In my own life, and in my work with senior leaders in organizations all over the world, I have found that it can change our lives to get curious about our fallback and about the characters that storm the stage when we are losing ourselves. Not only to understand that there are ways we fall out of our highest capacities, not only to attempt to be gracious with that occasional fall—but to see why we are falling and how that fall is not just a misery but a gift.

Take Maya, a senior leader in a large technology company. She noticed that when she was presenting to the executive team (her boss and his colleagues, as well as the CEO), she often lost some of the capacities that she was famous for in other contexts. She became deep in the details, and when people asked her to climb up to a more strategic level, she simply couldn't. "I know exactly what I should be doing," she told me. "I teach this to other people all the time. And I know what our strategy is and can talk about it at any level you need. But not in that room I can't. In that room I get down in the weeds, and strategic thinking simply does not arrive in my head."

It's not that Maya lacks the skills to do what is required. It's that in this particular context, she loses those skills. And, as she and I looked at this phenomenon, we discovered that it wasn't just in that boardroom that she experienced fallback. It was when she went to visit her mother. When she became utterly overwhelmed with her young family at home. She began to see glimpses of this "Drowning in Details" character in most of the stressful places in her life. And, instead of figuring out how to never feel that way again, Maya poured a cup of tea and sat down with this character—about whom she had previously felt only shame. She learned to understand what Drowning in Details was taking care of, where she came from. And next time she stood in front of the executive team, she was able to ensure that she was enough on top of the details so Drowning in Details could take a step back and Maya the strategic one could take a step forward.

As Maya explored her fallback along the path this book will teach you to walk, three amazing things happened.

First, she could see herself more honestly. Instead of imagining that this thing that was happening to her was either entirely her fault (I'm so embarrassed!) or entirely the fault of others (the executive team is so rude to those of us who come and present!), she was able to look at herself cleanly and to describe exactly what was going on for her. Because of that clear look, she could expand out from the particulars of any individual moment of fallback and see where else that character showed up. Seeing the character in multiple places helped Maya get a bigger view on herself and on her context.

Second, this bigger view removed the shame Maya had felt every time she left the executive team meetings and the blame she had felt every time she argued fiercely with her partner at home. Maya could look at Drowning in Details with compassion and even empathy, noticing how Drowning in Details had emerged from Maya's childhood as the eldest of her siblings and how useful she had been when Maya was growing up in a single-mother household.

Finally, this clearer and more empathetic look allowed Maya to begin to make slightly different choices, to notice when Drowning in Details was likely to come and to offer her some support as well as learn from her what was necessary. She discovered that at first she still needed to make a detailed plan and bring a detailed PowerPoint presentation with her to the executive team meetings, but she made sure to not show the slides and instead she led a more strategic conversation. As long as she knew she could handle the details, she didn't need to prove it to others quite so much.

And so this is what the fallback investigation offers us. Theoretically, this inquiry turns some of what we have believed about adult development on its head. Adult developmentalists have argued back and forth about whether we regress. Val puts down this argument in the clarity of our own experiences. When we offer ourselves the time and space to inquire, we generally find there have been times when each of us has noticed a falling back into an earlier state, an evaporating of capacities that had—up until now—been our trusty companions. We might grow more complex as we develop, but that growth is not a simple one-way street, with our capacities accumulating like golden coins and stored in a vault. We grow our capacities and then, sometimes inexplicably, we lose them, the vault purloined and the door swinging on its hinges. And this redefinition of the two-way street of development makes the whole developmental story richer and more interesting. It makes those who have travelled far down the developmental pathway seem less like sophisticated creatures the rest of us can barely understand and more like fully fledged human beings in all of their messy splendour.

Practically, the investigation offers us a way out of the cycle of smallness and shame that fallback tends to create, offers us a chance to have tea with our smaller selves and put our arms around them. It offers us the chance to hold ourselves as whole and multifaceted. And it offers a series of techniques and practices that allow us to stumble back and sometimes catch ourselves rather than fall back and then dig ourselves deeper into the hole.

Personally, what Val has led me through over the years is a transformational journey of acceptance and love, not just for my own humanity but for the humanity of those around me. I have watched the caustic voice in my own head quiet as I have been able to (sometimes) shift from an inwardly-pointed rage to an inwardly-pointed love. Accepting myself even when I'm needy or angry or critical goes a long way toward accepting the less attractive parts of those I work and live with.

So now you get to join us. You'll get to peer inside the fallback of some marvelous humans inside these pages, and you'll get to peer inside yourself in a new way. It's time to lay down the weapons that you have used against yourself during times when you might have been falling back. Offer yourself the hand of forgiveness, the heart of acceptance, rather than the judgement of shame or guilt. Pour yourself a cup of tea, put on your best outfit, and meet your whole self—the biggest parts and the most fallen back. The complexity and disorientation of our world means that fallback is a part of our lives. Now is the time to understand ourselves in our messy but vibrant humanity and use our wholeness as a force for good.

INTRODUCTION

Here's the thing. In the *best* of times, you and me and everyone around us is going to show up in a way that does not embody the best version of self. We're going to say things we regret, lose patience with those we love more than life, fall into a funk that we wish even our cats didn't have to see, lash out in anger and sadness and fear, treat others poorly in protection of our own egos and identities, and then tell stories to others and ourselves that justify our actions, feelings, and thoughts. In short, we are going to fall back. *Fallback* is the loss of options, of capacity, of ability to feel, behave, and think at the emotional and psychological level that we are *normally* (read: *optimally*) capable. We are human, and as such we are incredibly complex and imperfect. And friend, these are decidedly not the best of times.

Yet, *because* we are human, we have the ability to grow and change, and be mindful and intentional about how this happens. We can cultivate the capacity to notice when we are not showing up as our best selves. We can be willing to be honest with ourselves about what's going on (even if we're not immediately honest with others). We can choose to not sink into blame or shame in an attempt to reject the pain and loss that will lurk in the shadows if we don't invite it into the light. We can seek to understand what it is that this aspect of self—an aspect that is as much *us* as the beauty—is trying to give us, to show us, to protect in us.

Still, the ego is powerful. It has many tricks for protecting itself and it's had a lifetime to cultivate this capacity. So this is going to require you to be patient, to hang in there when it just feels like crap, until you're able to discover what feels threatened in those moments, with that person, in that setting. And once you discover what it is that you hold dear, you can craft a more intentional, productive manner of protecting that value, of protecting self.

Fallback, when we recognize and accept it, can be about understanding when and why we are not able to bring our better self; about reframing our expectations of who we are in this world; about accepting the full messiness that is an inevitable component of being human; about coming to know and love a more authentic version of self; and about cultivating the environments for others to do the same.

This is the purpose of this book. This is the path to knowing a truer, messier, more honest and complex version of self—one that is more aligned with your purpose as a human. For you, this may be to become more comfortable in your own skin, to live with less shame or worry about the judgment of others, or for your life to be more consistently aligned with your values. Herein lie the means to unhooking the tethers that hold us to the story that was written for us, and that allow us to adjust the script to best reflect the person we wish to become.

Through this book, we will journey together to do just that.

In chapters 1 and 2 we will unpack the concept of development in adulthood and the phenomenon of fallback, both pointing to the fluidity of the ways in which we make sense of the world.

In chapter 3, you will be introduced to the three individuals who will serve as guides in your understanding of fallback throughout this book. As Diego, Robbin, and Octavia share their experiences of being in the grip of fallback, you will witness their pain and loss, glimpse the tethers pulling them back to an earlier part of self, and observe the loss of capacity, of other ways to see or act, that marks fallback.

In chapter 4, we will step into the warm glow of the ghost light that will illuminate our journey through the rest of the book as we use the metaphor of theater to discover the multiplicity of characters that comprise self.

In the middle chapters, you will become familiar with the mechanism of fallback and the process of forming a different relationship to it as you walk through the steps of noticing, reflecting, identifying triggers, recovering, and growing. You will see each of these steps play out in Diego's, Robbin's, Octavia's, and even my own experiences of leaving the ghost light burning for our fallback characters, thereby allowing us to form a different relationship with our fallback.

Alongside a theoretical and descriptive understanding of fallback and its relationship to how we grow as humans, you will be offered tools to enable you to better notice, reflect on, and understand your own experiences of and triggers for fallback, as well as strategies to more consistently show up in a way that better meets your intentions. Here is where the rubber will meet the road for you, as you are invited to explore your own experiences of fallback through a series of exercises.

The flow of chapters 5 through 16 is 1) this is what you need to know, 2) this is how this played out in another's experience, 3) this is how you can do this yourself.

In chapter 17, Diego, Robbin, and Octavia take the stage once more, articulating the plot twists that emerged through their illumination of fallback.

In chapter 18, we will explore the societal implications of fallback at the collective level, how we might enable its illumination and acceptance in organizations, and how fallback may be the descent toward healing that is needed at this time.

A decade ago, I articulated a theory for understanding fallback informed by my research with key thinkers in the fields of adult development and leadership development—William Torbert, Robert Kegan, Susanne Cook-Greuter, Jennifer Garvey Berger, Chuck Palus, and David McCallum. You will find their voices intermingled with my own throughout the book. And in the afterword, Torbert, Berger, Palus, and McCallum accompany me as we revisit our understanding and continue to fence the field of fallback through a theoretical exploration of its criteria and distinctions.

While there are many books that focus on the ecstasy of growing into a fuller version of self, this book shines a light on the inevitable pain and loss that accompanies the journey of human becoming, of uncovering the fullest and most complex version of your self. This exploration allows us to recognize the fluidity and multi-dimensionality of the self; the influence of context (place, time, others on their own path to becoming) on who we are able to bring to the table; the gifts that can only be received from a place of surrender into those earlier but still very present and important aspects of self; and how seeking out and accepting the gifts of fallback can allow us to recover, grow, and more intentionally align with our intentions.

There are many circumstances that we humans face that bring us to our knees at the precipice of our sense-making:[1] in our marriages, our friendships, our parenting, and our organizational lives. The implications of undertaking this process of discovery and growth are many, not the least of which is the opportunity it offers us to acknowledge the full range of who we are as humans.

This allows us a more compassionate *knowing* of others who also traverse the path of human becoming, rife with wretched potholes and glorious vistas, uphill trudges and hair-whipping-in-the-wind sprints. For, once we are able to recognize that we are truly in the process of becoming—we are moving, not still—we are able to loosen our grip on a version of one's self that has been written for us. We are able to see the possibilities that lie in embracing the full and fluid complexity of showing up in this world as a human, and to allow others to do so, as well.

Without an understanding of fallback—a way to notice it, reflect on it, recover, and potentially grow from it—the darkness that accompanies a greater knowing of self as one develops can be overwhelming and stunting. With an understanding of fallback, we are given a gift, a tool, to help us suss out the most profound values and purposes we hold, and a path to showing up in greater alignment with these.

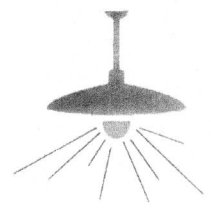

CHAPTER 1
THE FLUIDITY OF DEVELOPMENT

Early in my doctoral program, I encountered adult development theory. Most of us have some familiarity with child development theory, but theories of adult development are lesser known. The prevailing assumption up until about forty-five years ago was that once we stopped growing physically, we stopped growing altogether. A few pioneers built upon the work of child developmentalists like Jean Piaget to articulate and test a theory of adult development—our capacity to continue to grow cognitively, emotionally, egoically, and spiritually even after our physical development has ceased.

These theorists, including Jane Loevinger, William Torbert, Robert Kegan, and Susanne Cook-Greuter, are constructive developmentalists. That is, they believe that humans are not simply predetermined by the stimuli they encounter, but rather actively participate in constructing their reality in the context of their environments. Similar to child development, the tenets of constructive developmental theory state that we develop through stages of increasing complexity and that development is forward-moving and inclusive of the prior stages that we have grown through. Moreover, the adult developmentalists hold that there can be substantive, enduring shifts in how adults come to know and re-know the world. The theory of adult development aims to articulate and predict the patterns of human growth that are possible throughout adulthood.

Rooms in a House

One way to think about development is to imagine that you have a house with many rooms. In the earlier stages of development, you have access to only a few of these rooms. In fact, you don't even realize that other rooms exist. You think you opted into a one-bedroom, one-bath unit with a kitchen and living room.

As time goes on, you realize that there's a door in your house that you've never noticed. You're curious about what's behind this door, but it's locked, so you begin to strategize how to open it. Over time, you make some progress. You discover a set of keys, so you try each of the keys and eventually one works. But the door still won't open. It's as if something is blocking it. So you keep pushing up against that door, perhaps tentatively at first. Then with more force. What is behind here? And might I really need it?

Over time, after many attempts to open the door to the closed-off room, exhaustion sets in. Or frustration. Or doubt and a tinge of fear. You start to wonder what that room—a potential Pandora's box—might hold. And you begin to think, *I've been pretty comfortable here with my bedroom, kitchen, living room, and bath setup. I'm good.* So, for a time, you settle back into the space that you have, the one that you opted into those many years before.

Before long, curiosity gets the best of you. Or maybe you really do begin to feel the confines of your smaller space, and think, *I could sure use more square footage.* So you go back and push on that door a little bit harder. And eventually, you're able to open that door enough to poke your head through the opening and get a glimpse into the room.

What a discovery! This room has a distinct style, unique colors and patterns, new furniture, different tools. "There's that thingamabob I've been looking for!" You exert more effort to get the door open and acquire a solid standing in the room. You become enchanted as you explore.

Across the room, you see a window and when you gaze out, you see things outside of your house that you never noticed before. You see, the windows in the other rooms of your house face a different direction. Through this window, you're looking out on a beautiful tree that is blooming. You see a dead patch of grass that the sprinkler doesn't seem to be reaching. And wait a minute! There's a trailhead that you didn't know existed.

You turn around and look back through the doorway to the other parts of the house—the rooms you've lived in all these years. Suddenly, you see these rooms and what's inside of them from a completely different perspective. You notice things in and about those old rooms for the first time. Perhaps you notice that the first couch you bought has now become a bit thread-bare. Perhaps you notice the artwork on the walls looks a bit dated, a reflection of a former sense of style that now feels off. Then you see your favorite chair, the one you love to cuddle up and read in, and look at it longingly because you know it's been a place of solace for you in the past.

And so it goes as you discover and expand into more and more rooms of your developmental house over time. These rooms allow you access to a different way of seeing things within the house of self; a different way of seeing things outside the house. Similarly, as we develop into greater complexity, we have access to more options and different perspectives on what's both inside and external to us. And those earlier things—the house that we first took up occupancy in with the original rooms—still exist. And they still have tremendous value. You certainly still need a kitchen and a bathroom. But you have this expansive other space that offers you new capacities, additional perspectives, and increased options.

The Nonlinear Nature of Development

When I encountered adult development theory early in my doctoral program, it felt so freeing to see that there had been some sort of path in my life toward...well, something other than what had been before. To see that there was more that lay in front of me. To be able to make sense of my self through a framework that spoke to me and my experience of human becoming so clearly.

Except for one little thing. My path toward learning, growth, and greater complexity had not always been so linear, onward, and upward.

You see, while the theory contained hints at a more fluid movement up *and* down the spectrum of developmental capacity, the idea that we may occasionally not have access to our fullest level of sense-making—to all of the rooms in our developmental house that we had heretofore unlocked—was not explicit.

Certainly, the theorists addressed how we experience a seesaw motion back and forth between the stage that has held us and the one that is emerging as we transition to the next stage of development. And those who are really interested in the fine print of the theory would find that there are several incremental weigh stations along the road from one stage to the next.

In fact, we are very rarely solidly in one stage. We live most of our lives in transition between set, distinct levels of development. The lines that would seem to bifurcate our capacity for sense-making according to the handy stages and definitions of the theory are in real life blurred, with "us" being on the way from the prior and to the next delineated stages, with one shoulder through the doorway that we are trying mightily to disjar.

It makes sense that all of the mile markers, with their accompanying directional signage, were not so prominently featured in what is a very complex theory. Presenting development as set, distinct levels of growth makes it more understandable. Yet as a result, developmental theory is often portrayed as a stairway-to-heaven type experience—one in which we stand solidly on one step or the next, solidly in one room or another.

As I dug into an exploration of fallback with the key thinkers who comprised my dissertation research think tank, one of them, Chuck Palus, a master of metaphors, offered a different perspective. In our conversations, he examined what is referred to in the field as one's *center of gravity* developmental stage. The center of gravity is meant to point to the developmental place from which one makes meaning most of the time, and this is generally described as a particular stage with a specific corresponding definition.

In Chuck's pondering, he explored what our physical center of gravity looks like on a staircase. He explained that when we are walking up a set of stairs, our head might be furthest out in front, torso leaning slightly forward of our hips, one leg trailing behind. In the process of ascending that staircase, we are very fleetingly, if at all, solidly upright—head-over-shoulders-over-waist-over-knees-over-feet. In fact, to maintain our center of gravity on the incline, we must necessarily have weight distributed along the plane in order to not topple over. Similarly, in our developmental movement, we are very rarely solidly on one "stair" or in one room, or, as it were, in one stage. There can be a part of us pushing forward toward what we call our *leading edge*. And there is also a part that lags behind, still held in balance by a prior way of knowing and seeing the world.[1]

To say that my own experience of development was marked by a perfect-postured and consistent center-of-gravity stage of development would be laughable. While I knew that I could at times get to the "peak" of my developmental capability, I realized that there were so many more times when I settled into the plateaus of my capacity, and other times, much more frequent than I wanted to admit, that I experienced significant disequilibrium, sinking deep into the valley of my sense-making and acting.

So where was this in the theory? Was I some sort of statistical anomaly? Or was there something lying in the shadows that needed to be brought into the light in order to paint the full landscape of our developmental terrain?

I found something that was incredibly unsettling in myself that I could not make sense of through the literature, and I set out to find the answer. Bill Torbert had referenced a phenomenon that he called fallback in development.[2] David McCallum was the first to document empirically the experience of fallback in individuals at each of the levels of development. Fallback, also referred to as "temporary regression" in McCallum's research, described the experience of temporarily not being able to access one's most complex capacity for sense-making and acting.[3]

It is from this mile marker that I embarked to discover all I could about fallback. I was fortunate to have six fellow inquirers accompany me on my expedition as the "key thinkers" in my dissertation research. William Torbert, Susanne Cook-Greuter, and Robert Kegan are three of the original pioneers in the mapping of adult development theory. Jennifer Garvey Berger, well-studied in the developmental maps articulated by Kegan, Torbert, and Cook-Greuter, expanded upon their use and application with her work to help individuals and organizations cultivate leadership. As noted, David McCallum was the first to empirically observe fallback in his own research exploring adaptive self-scaffolds, the behaviors that help individuals engage challenges with intention and purpose.[4] And Chuck Palus had spent his career developing leadership programs informed by a curiosity about the intersection of multiple disciplines—adult development, leadership, and beyond.

The wisdom and knowledge of these six greatly shaped my own understanding of how humans develop over the lifespan and the role that fallback plays in their development. Nearly a decade following my original research with these key thinkers, we would reconvene as I neared completion of the research for this book to explore what we were still curious about as we considered the phenomenon of fallback (see afterword), bumped up against it in our own lives, accompanied others in their experiences, and faced into an ever more uncertain world in which our individual and our collective fallback was calling for address (see chapter 18).[5]

During our recent convening, Palus considered the ways in which the positivist framing of development as a journey toward enlightenment has infiltrated our practice in unhelpful ways. He referenced the writing of Elaine Herdman-Barker and Nancy Wallis, who note the desire of organizations to have their people transform to the most complex level of development, thereby equipping them with the full suite of developmental capacities. Palus summarized the example they offer, explaining, "Especially these days, it seems like it's the imperative of the people. *We want our people to be at the Transforming stage. Yep, that's it. Look at this list of virtues.* Lawrence Kohlberg called it the bag of virtues. Organizational leaders just see this whole checklist and think, *If all people could do this, that would be great.* And then somebody who's clearly been scored at a Transforming level[6] behaves badly in a meeting and otherwise exhibits a whole host of frustrating personality characteristics, and they're kind of amazed. *What happened?* Here's the quote: 'I thought that by transforming, all such glitches would have been ironed out.'"[7]

Palus continued, "And of course, we know that's not the case. We don't lose all our glitches. We don't lose the primitive stuff in our personality just by being at a later stage. So, I really like that as a corrective. Because as scholars, academics, and consultants, we shy away from the mystery and the enigmas. We want our clients to know that there's research, and there's a model, and they can depend on the model, and quote the model. But if we tell them, 'Well, it's a lot messier than that,' then that's often difficult."

McCallum agreed, noting the disconnect that people experience when their push toward development doesn't yield them the sweetness-and-light experience that they were aiming for. He posited, "The obsession with moving forward and getting to the later stages has been very harmful; and the degree of self-idealization, which then just creates more neurosis and unhappiness. And I'll notice that in myself, as I think over the years. I think about my idea when I first started studying development. *Oh my gosh, this is going to solve everything if we can get everybody down the conveyor belt.* Certainly, this point around how can I just step into my more compassionate self? It might be in some ways the healthier question for a lot of us to ask ourselves and others."[8]

While development opens up more options, allows us to see ourselves more clearly, and gives us more tools, there's also incredible pain and loss in the truthful seeing. As McCallum noted, the later stages are not the promised land. And not being *there* does not make you bad, or less than, or incapable.

We say this often in the field of adult development. "Later is not better. We must transcend *and* include." Nonetheless, there is a tendency in this positivist field to only focus on the "bag of virtues" that is yours for the taking at the later developmental stages. In our sales pitch for development, we implicitly denigrate the earlier stages and with them the earlier parts of self that are still very present in our cast of characters. And we fail to really appreciate the gifts that that earlier self has to offer…to us and others.

Palus appreciated our colleagues Herdman-Barker and Wallis naming the complexity of what it is to be human. He explained, "Elaine and Nancy sort of poke at the elephant in the room in our field, which is that human development is 'exquisitely complicated.'[9] People are exquisitely complicated. They're recognizing 'the essential messiness and mystery,'[10] and the 'contextualized, dissonant, enigmatic nature of human development.'[11]"

Our orientation—in the field of adult development, in the practice of leadership development—is to the top of the mountain. Fallback runs counter to the prevailing leaning in the field, and the one we often perpetuate with those we support along their developmental journeys, that the answer to all life's problems will be found if we race to the later developmental stages. By orienting this way, we fail to secure a solid base upon which the terrain of our development can be built. Palus and McCallum cautioned us take heed of the false promises of rapid ascension to the pinnacle of our development. Fallback offers us the opportunity to solidify that base.

CHAPTER 2
WHAT IS FALLBACK?

You know in those old 80s adventure or sci-fi flicks when the walls start closing in around the protagonist? Think *Indiana Jones* and *Star Wars*. Doorways close, a boulder rolls in to block the entrance to the cave, windows disappear behind the shifting walls. All the while, the protagonist is desperate for a way to escape the impending doom and is forced to become smaller and smaller in an effort to avoid being crushed by the shrinking space they are in.

Well, this doesn't just happen in movies. It happens in our psychological self when we experience fallback. Fallback is when individuals unintentionally make meaning from an earlier stage of development than is their center-of-gravity, meaning-making structure. During fallback, there is a temporary absence of all other options to think, feel, or behave differently. When we are triggered into fallback, it feels very much like the walls are closing in around us, seemingly forcing us to become smaller in order to survive. The doors and windows that provided options and outlets before fast disappear. The possibilities that lay beyond them are no longer able to be seen or grasped. We go into survival mode, seizing the weapons that are in our psychological reach without evaluating if they are the best defense for the situation, or even if a defense is truly needed.

A prominent context for my own fallback is in my relationship with my children. The combination of my striving for perfection—

my own and theirs—along with the baggage of my own childhood often makes for a situation rife with hope but peppered with the landmines planted by my expectations. An example....

> I picked up the kids from the home of our family friend Leah with whom they had enjoyed a sleepover. A breakfast outing was to be our last little adventure before I left on a four-night writing retreat. I had been assigned a special project at work that had exponentially grown in scope and already caused me to delay the retreat and cancel planned time off with the family. It had been a busy couple of weeks, and I hadn't spent much quality time, indeed much time at all, with the kids. I wanted to before I was gone for a few days.
>
> Leah was planning to come to breakfast with us, but after a 4:47 a.m. wake-up call by my then one-year-old, she declined. I was already anticipating the worst. I hadn't had much sleep the past few weeks. I'd been short on patience, cranky, and hadn't had much capacity to deal with anything that wasn't going well. But I wanted to do something special for the kids. Going to breakfast with my mom was such a special event when I was little. I wanted my kids to have this experience, this special memory. So we went.
>
> Townsend (at the time, five years old) got out of the car first and immediately threw his bag on the ground. I can't remember why he was upset. He needed to share something with his sister? He was told he couldn't go to the playground? He, too, hadn't had much sleep during his sleepover. I grabbed him by the arm and told him to pick up his things immediately. "If you can't get it together and behave, we are not going to breakfast. We will go straight home. And if you behave like this in the restaurant, regardless of where we are in our meal, we will get up and leave. Do you understand?" Grave head nodding. We were not off to a great start on my quest for joyful memory-making.
>
> Into the restaurant we went, and I immediately thought, maybe I should call my husband Sonnie to meet us. But I knew Sonnie didn't want to meet us, and this was supposed to be my special time with the kids. (Insert expectations that none of us were well-equipped to meet.)

Neither child had eaten, and they were both hungry. Sloane, like most one-year-olds, didn't want to sit in her highchair and screamed to make her discontent known. Toys and menus flew from the table. I grabbed Sloane's arm, hard, and commanded through gritted teeth, "Stop this now!" Townsend tried to hug me, but I refused to acknowledge his outreach. He retreated, dejected.

Disgust, not empathy, filled me. I was angry at my kids for not behaving as I thought they should; angry at the waitstaff for not delivering our food quicker. I enumerated all variety of threats if they couldn't get it together. Tears sprouted from my eyes as shame and judgment—of myself, of the kids, of the people around us—simmered inside of me and eventually cascaded in a flood of tears. We stormed out, food half eaten, me holding tightly to arms, placing Sloane roughly in her car seat.

Rage exuded from every part of my body. As I tried to fasten my own seatbelt, it stuck. It thinks there's a wreck. There is. It's me. "Breathe," I silently told myself. But I didn't want to breathe.

"Get in the house," I ordered as I brought the car to an abrupt stop in the driveway. Once inside, I plopped Sloane on the floor, turned on my heel, and slammed the door behind me as I stormed outside.

Escape. I needed to run away. But I couldn't escape from the thing that I wished to flee—me. This expression of my worst self was more than I could bear. And what I was leaving on was guilt, regret, sadness, shame.

Fallback—the complete loss of options, of capacity, of access to feel, to behave, to think at the developmental level at which you are ideally capable. A self exists—at least when the birds are chirping, the breeze is blowing, the sun is shining—that does have options, capacity, and access. But you put me, filled with my highest expectations and my lowest physiological and psychological capacities (resulting from exhaustion, stress, and hunger) in a public place with my young children with their own limited developmental and physiological capacities, and all of a sudden, you have one supposed grown-up and two children with near about the same in-the-moment developmental capacity.

Remember that metaphor of development as ever-expanding access to the rooms in our developmental house? That was inspired by developmental theorist Jennifer Garvey Berger as we explored the phenomenon of fallback. Berger described fallback as being in a house with a bunch of rooms, rooms that you had access to up until that point. You go to open the door to these rooms (in reality, you frantically claw at the doorknobs) only to find that they are locked. And for this period—be it seconds, days, weeks, months, or years—you are on lockdown, with only the resources of certain "rooms" within your reach.[1]

The locked rooms Berger references are those aspects of self that are bigger, more spacious, able to hold more nuance, complexity, and options. These are the rooms to which your "normal" developmental center of gravity—the place from which you have the capacity to make sense, feel, and act—grants you access. Fallback is an unconscious loss of these capacities. Your all-access pass to the rooms in your developmental house has been suspended…until further notice. For now, you are stuck within the confines of the developmental stage to which you have fallen back. And stuck and confined are exactly how I felt in this episode with my children.

I had this ideal in my head, bolstered by a happy memory from my childhood. I gripped tightly to expectations I had put upon myself to be the kind of mom that has joyful moments in public places with her children. I clearly had a script (though I didn't realize it at the time) for how this scene would play out.

I would inquire about their sleepover. They would regale me with stories about their adventures. We would giggle and tell jokes. Our hearts would be filled, and we could take a mental snapshot of this beautiful moment and file it away in our memories to reflect lovingly upon.

When I'm at my best, these beautiful moments do happen. Or at least I have more capacity to deal with them when they inevitably go off script. At times when I'm able to bring my bigger self, I also have more capacity to see the beauty in the imperfection. I can have compassion for the tremendous impact of exhaustion on little (and big) bodies and minds. I can be flexible when Sloane wants to sit in my lap when she eats breakfast. I can distract my children with my own playfulness to lighten the mood. Or I can recognize that this just isn't meant to be today and change plans.

But as the winds of real life began to pick up and the rain began to wash away my children's and my own developmental capacities, the doors of the rooms that held my bigger capacities began to slam shut. What I wanted more than anything was to protect my vision for how this scene would play out. Because if we couldn't do this, if we couldn't have one hour together in a restaurant that was pleasant, what kind of mom was I? And what kind of kids were they?

The more the doors of the house slammed shut, the more desperate I was to control the situation. The more desperate I was to control, the deeper into the basement of my development I went. *Breathe, Valerie.* But I didn't want to breathe. Then, not only the doors to the rooms were closing, but the storm shutters too. I could see what was happening. I was being swept back and down, and I was bound and determined to take everyone and everything down with me. It was all or nothing. And if it wasn't going to be perfect, I was sure as hell going to make it a perfect storm.

Often when we experience fallback, we circle the wagons, hunker down. What these metaphors conjure is a feeling that we need to protect something that is important to us, that we value, that feels at risk, but we very rarely experience or articulate it as such. We dismiss the way we show up in fallback, this aspect of self that is smaller than we like to see ourselves, than we like to be seen as. Often, for me this first shows up as blame of others. In the crumbling that happens with time and honest reflection, it shows up as shame of self.

There's much that can and does happen in this space, be it the stories we tell ourselves, the stories others tell us, or both. These storytellers, others and self included, may weave the following tales:

- The supportive self/friend: "Girl, you were justified! Those damn entitled kids. Here they'd had a fun sleepover with a friend, and you were trying to do something nice for them by taking them out to breakfast."
- The brush-it-off self/friend: "Those are such hard ages for kids (and their parents). I remember I didn't dare enter a restaurant with my kids until they were over the age of eight!"
- The technical-fix self/friend: "Kids need to behave. It's your job to teach them limits and follow through. Have you read *Love and Logic?*"

- The judging self/friend: "OH.MY.GOSH. You did what? Did anyone see? You must have been horrified! Have you thought about seeing a therapist to get your anger under control?"
- The exhausted-with-this-pattern self/husband who is ambushed by this upon your return home: "Val, why do you even try to do these things when you know how this is going to turn out? Try to have a little patience with them. Try to let go." And let me tell you, my husband's perspective (and the judgment I hear in it) are the last things that are going to help me return to calm. Very likely because I know he is right. I know he knows me and can anticipate how these things are going to play out. Yet I persist in spite of what I know.

Whatever the story, it feels awful and constricting, and our thoughts go immediately to how we can break free. The problem with this *get me out of here* knee-jerk response to be, feel, and act better quick is that we end up rejecting a part of us that may not be pretty but is still very much us.

Often, when we experience fallback, something feels threatened that is incredibly important to us. Yet, when we reject the fallback—our thoughts, our behavior, our experience of it—we shut down the possibility of being in inquiry with fallback, of uncovering what it is we value that we, in our fallback, are protecting. Our task is to figure out what it is. Our task is to shine light into the shadow in order to reveal the gift it has to offer. With the key of the lesson, the grace, in hand, we will be better equipped to recover, to unlock the doors that have shut off parts of our full self; and, perhaps, the key will allow us to enter new rooms to which we haven't had access before. We come to know our selves better, more authentically, more truthfully. This knowing offers other possibilities for what may be next.

In the next chapter, through the stories shared by Robbin, Diego, and Octavia, you will experience the in-the-grip-ness of fallback, witness its expression, its texture, the range of ways it presents in contexts ranging from parenthood and pandemics to relational and organizational strife.

Let us take our seats. The show is about to begin.

CHAPTER 3
PROLOGUE
MEET DIEGO, ROBBIN, AND OCTAVIA

Diego

Diego and Kyra were in love. The electricity between them flowed at many levels: body, spirit, and mind.

Diego and Kyra were also married…to other people. Kyra and her husband Brock had thought of their marriage as "mostly monogamous." Brock had long known and accepted that Kyra could not be held solely by one person. Only once before had one of Kyra's many deep friendships turned to romance, but Brock was accustomed to Kyra's openness to love in its many forms. In fact, he loved that about her and was surprisingly unthreatened by it all. However, Kyra's connection with a partner outside of their union had never before been quite so multi-faceted as it was with Diego. Nonetheless, Brock had been accommodating in an attempt to keep things together.

Diego and his wife, Ellie, had an agreement that allowed them to enjoy themselves sexually outside of their marriage, as long as it didn't get into marriage-breaking territory. In other words, as long as neither of them fell in love. Diego and Ellie lived a wonderful life and loved each other. She was an excellent wife and mother to their children. Their marriage was perfect. At least that's what Diego and Ellie thought. It was true that their marriage, in many ways, served their needs very well. They were good parents and playmates together. Diego recalled, "I didn't know any better. And to Ellie, it was perfect."

Then Diego met Kyra. Diego realized that what had been missing in his relationship with Ellie was intimacy in the form of deep conversation, curiosity, and exploration of who each individual was at their core—and who they were together. He fell in love with Kyra unexpectedly, hard. What bothered Ellie was not that Diego had slept with Kyra, but that he had fallen in love with her.

Diego described the dynamics as a system of four. He and Kyra worked hard to hold onto love and closeness with their spouses as well as with one another. Their marital partners had significantly different responses, with Brock trying to keep things from breaking, and Ellie doing all she could to shake Kyra out of the system. After two years, Ellie had had enough and gave Diego an ultimatum—me or Kyra.

Diego told Kyra, "We need to make a choice in the next three days." In that time, Kyra and Brock revisited their agreement and decided upon an arrangement that would allow Kyra and Diego to continue their relationship, and Kyra and Brock to continue their marriage. Yet, what Diego was looking for was a choice along the lines of what Ellie had demanded from him. Me or Brock? He sought certainty, clarity, and timelines. Kyra didn't offer any of these.

The ultimatum that Diego received from Ellie that would have him choosing between continuing a life with her and their family or pursuing a life with Kyra tipped both Diego and his conception of his relationship with Kyra out of balance. Before the ultimatum, Diego had embraced the unforced emergence of his relationship with Kyra. The openness, the lack of clarity, the shades of grey that Diego had accepted in his relationship with Kyra in the past suddenly became no longer welcome. Kyra and Brock continued to operate in the space of non-definition, a relational system that existed beyond the confines of social conventions that define marriage and partnership and impose monogamy.

The "ideal" Diego could make sense of complexity, could see the texture in situations, and could blend power and love seamlessly. Diego, however, was far from his ideal self in this circumstance. In this moment, with Ellie demanding a black-and-white choice—Ellie or Kyra—Diego, too, was seeking a black-and-white response. Kyra, pirouetting along the greyscale, didn't offer the clarity that he wanted. Kyra's response sent him tumbling down.

Diego said, "I was prepared to choose Kyra. And I wanted Kyra to be clear on what she was prepared to commit to. And Kyra is Kyra. She's much swirlier than I am, and much less in the world of black-and-white than my wife cares for. I fell back into my small self, seeing things in black-and-white, and wanting to be dealt with in terms of certainty and win/lose that I have been comfortable with. Self-orientation took hold of me, and I reverted instinctively to using unilateral forms of power. In that place, I lost perspective, I saw no options. I found it impossible to see where the other person was coming from, impossible to find a handle back into my bigger self. I went for the kill instinctively."

Diego's fallback was triggered by Kyra's response, which wasn't a wholesale reciprocal choosing of him and rejection of Brock. At least that's what the external trigger was. This external trigger ignited dynamics within Diego that had been dormant for some time. The fear of loss was a common denominator.

"I was losing a bunch of things," Diego explained. "Immediately, I was losing the dream of a life with Kyra. And that has many dimensions to it: a big professional dimension, a writing dimension, and a romantic dimension. Then in the aftermath, I thought that I was losing myself. I thought I was losing my inner compass, that my inner compass was somehow wrong, that the pieces that held it together were misguided, misoriented."

The internal triggers that were set off by Kyra's swirly response to Diego's pleading for black-and-white certainty were also characterized by fear. Diego feared not being in control, not winning, making a choice that could lead to loneliness in old age. When these triggers collided, they sparked Diego's impulse to score a point to get even.

Diego realized that this was not a one-off pattern for him, as a whole range of experiences in his history began to string together. Diego referred to his fears of not being in control and not winning as "the usual suspects." Diego observed, "I've been reliving that same story under various guises in different circumstance of my life, and every single time, I thought of it as an individual isolated story." He poetically referred to this well-known experience of fallback as "the isolated story that I have been rewriting."

Robbin

"The last time I went into work was Thursday, March 12, 2020," Robbin remembered. "My wife was being worked like crazy, which spilled over into the next day, which spilled over into the whole weekend. I was bracing for a long few days of my wife being overworked and me needing to take a backseat. But then it became clear that school wouldn't be happening for a good long time. And without school, work wasn't going to be happening. And my wife needed to work for the sake of the country."

The Covid-19 pandemic had arrived and brought with it the lockdown of a nation.

On March 13, 2020, schools in Robbin's city were closed for two weeks. Robbin's five-year-old son Charles's last year of preschool had abruptly come to a halt without anyone yet realizing that a brief break would turn into a monthslong readjustment. Robbin's daughter, Elsa, had been in the care of an in-home nanny who retreated into the confines of her own sequestered household when the city and the nation shut down.

As the world went into lockdown, individuals in every corner of the globe were forced to figure out how to simultaneously tend to their day jobs while also moonlighting as full-time caregivers and educators to their children. There was no option for Robbin's wife to divert her time and attention to the second full-time job of caring for their children. Linda, a congressional legislative staffer, was working sixteen-hour days writing emergency legislation to stave off the financial collapse of individuals, businesses, cities, and states during the pandemic. The task of childcare fell squarely on Robbin's shoulders.

As agency, certainty, control, and a sense of who Robbin had previously known himself to be seemed evermore beyond his grasp, Robbin clung to what seemed within his reach in an attempt to hold onto some aspect of his professional identity and some glimmer of a self that fed his soul. Robbin recalled, "In the first few days and weeks, I was desperately longing to have expansive conversations, to shed light on things that seem intractable, to provide company and comfort to others through conversations." Expansive conversations that shed light while providing company and comfort were regular aspects of Robbin's reality and key to his identity B.C.–Before Covid.

But when the pandemic took hold, Robbin's context shrunk without warning and, with it, his identity. Day-after-day, possibility frittered away. Robbin noted, "With the prospect of being in communion and fellowship with other people, there was a threat of obliteration. So I did close off more. I kept feeling smaller and smaller and desperately trying to do things to overcompensate for the conversations that weren't happening and to stay alive, like cooking intricate things. But it wasn't cutting it. After the goal of being in touch with others in the professional milieu was adjusted from one a day to maybe a weekly conversation to nothing, I became grouchy and short-fused."

The structures that had propped up Robbin's bigger self were shuttered, and with them the person he had known himself to be. Robbin recalled, "As life shrank, I didn't have the ability to wake up. Suddenly I'm not around grown-ups having big spacious conversations. Suddenly I'm doing three meals a day. And if I try to focus on my five-year-old son and read with him, my nearly two-year-old daughter wants to be put on the potty because she knows that that guarantees attention." Robbin continued, "I was just so focused on getting kids and family through the day. The thing that was missing for me was this sense of purpose that I execute by working."

Soon the effort of bringing himself to the things Robbin loved and that he knew would help lift him out of the abyss of fallback seemed too much of an investment. Robbin explained, "I just ran out of energy. I started making calculations like if clients want to book my time, I'll take it, but I'm not going to be proactive about reaching out and getting hours on the calendar. A few weeks into it, I realized that I would have whole weeks without a single coaching session."

This was made all the more painful as he watched colleagues seizing the opportunity to support people in this unprecedented time of crisis. "I remember during the second week of March saying to a colleague, 'This is the biggest coaching opportunity ever!' Of course, this was before I realized the scope and magnitude," Robbin recalled. "I fell apart. My colleague is off revolutionizing the world of coaching in a way that is awe inspiring. And I thought, let me just put myself off market."

As the groundhog days of Robbin's pandemic existence repeated, he began to feel less and less like himself and more like a repertoire of characters from his upbringing. He recalled, "There was my yelling grandfather. There was my spiteful dad. There was my suck-it-up-and-make-food grandma. It's suddenly having those people sticking their hands up my backside and having me be a puppet. It's an identity thing. It feels like I'm not me. I'm someone else, and I don't really like him."

"When these characters came on the scene, what felt at risk was control," noted Robbin. "Whenever I felt like I couldn't get things right, I would get short-tempered. The overcorrection was just a loud self-assertion."

Robbin could sometimes see that his perspective had become stuck and narrow and that something else existed. Yet he was unable to grasp what that could be or how to enact it. "It felt like I'm hemmed in. This is all I've got. And I could see that stuff over there, and I don't have access to it. There was a spaciousness that I took for granted in my mind, in my physicality, that wasn't there. It was just kind of a walls closing in, trapped kind of feeling."

"I vividly remember during the early weeks of lockdown, Elsa, my almost two-year-old daughter, punched me in the face. And I started screaming." Robbin admitted, "I felt like there was a failure on my part to be a good, functioning dad even after I had made what felt like these gigantic sacrifices. Like, I don't get to be this grown-up. I don't get to be the guy who has these wonderful conversations that change people's lives. When I do have conversations, they're with people whose rationality hasn't yet come online and it's very frustrating. And they punch me?"

Robbin observed, "I was also desperate because, sure these munchkins love me, but they don't see in me what I see and prize in myself." And these munchkins were Robbin's primary companions for months on end, with little respite for him to encounter the parts of self that he had known, that felt vanquished. "There is a productive drive that was frustrated in those days and weeks. And I think I-produce-therefore-I-am is part of a certain condition that I experienced. And I wasn't producing, therefore that was at risk—the *I am* part."

In despair and longing for a different way of being with no energy or capacity to get there, Robbin became increasingly self-focused, consumed by his own experience of loss and sacrifice. Robbin's experience during the onset of the pandemic and lockdown was Robbin against the world, Robbin against his wife, Robbin against his kids. Soon, he would add to the list of opponents his commercial landlord.

As Robbin saw his professional identity dissolving, when it became clear that a return to the office was not in the cards, was not even legally permitted, Robbin attempted unsuccessfully to terminate the lease for his office space. He vacated the space, but when the landlord asked him to pay the rent on the remainder of his lease, Robbin felt both his security and his identity were in freefall.

Later, Robbin shared, "I became vengeful, and I lashed out. I roared with blind rage at one of the poor property managers who was tasked with engaging with me. I accused her of wanting to bleed me dry. It felt like a physical threat. No income. You guys are charging me. What the fuck?" Robbin had been done wrong, and he needed to push against that.

Robbin described himself as "crotchety" with "middle fingers raised." "I was trying to code my own thoughts and figure out do I care about what other people see when they see me. And it was a very clear, *Fuck that! No!* For me to feel on purpose, for me to be against the world, there's heavy engagement with others. But what others think had marginal bearing on my mindset." Robbin observed, "What was most important to me at the time was preservation, pure and simple."

This period of fallback, of which there would be several in the year to come, lasted seven weeks.

Octavia

"What if I pulled her hair?" wondered Octavia as she sat in a meeting with her colleagues as Brenda, the new division director, berated them. Brenda referred to the initiative Octavia had been leading as a gross failure in project management. She even used that language—"failure."

It had been only six weeks since Brenda had taken over the helm of Octavia's division at work. Even before she assumed her post, there were rumblings that Brenda, a thirty-year veteran of the organization, was a much different kind of manager than the former division director had been. Brenda had a reputation for her attention to detail, her broad-brush approach to every project and initiative, and her hierarchical orientation.

The prior division director was beloved by all. He was collaborative, had an eye on the big picture and the long game, and developed relationships marked by mutual respect and trust with every member of his team. Under the former director, the division was *the place* where employees wanted to work, not only because it was a happy place to be, but because they got their work done, and they did it well.

When the director left and Brenda took his place, Octavia's team held their breath in anticipation of the sea change that would accompany her arrival. Nonetheless, Octavia tried to keep an open mind. During the brief time that Brenda had been in her new role, Octavia had only passing encounters with her, primarily in the form of larger meetings. Before long, Brenda would become all too familiar with Octavia's work. Octavia had heard through the grapevine that Brenda had some criticisms of her work, but she hadn't heard directly from Brenda. Then a meeting was called.

"These videos are *awful!*" Brenda exclaimed in front of Octavia's boss and colleagues. "I've done videos in my other divisions. I'll show you examples. They were produced for the same amount of money, and they were *so much* better. That's the type of quality I'm looking for."

Octavia was incredulous. "I'm not incompetent! It's not like I don't have judgment," she thought. "I felt like I had to defend my credibility, almost like I had to save face or assert my competence. But there was this feeling of shame, too. Nobody wants to put out a crappy product. I think there was definitely a sense of doubt that came in. Then I was kind of angry that she had made me doubt myself for a minute, because I did not share her perspective."

Octavia remembered, "I could see that other people were feeling defensive. I was feeling defensive. It felt like a finger-wagging. We felt like we had been brought together to be taken to task." It seemed to Octavia as if Brenda was dead set on challenging relationships and weakening the teamwork and trust that had been a hallmark of the division to this point.

"I think what triggered me about Brenda was her use of power, the absolutes," observed Octavia. "She uses this very inflammatory, provocative language, like 'This is unacceptable. This is a failure in project management. The videos are just awful.'" Octavia believed Brenda was exercising unilateral power—not listening to people, seeking only to convey her own perspective. As the individuals working on the project offered context or explanation, it seemed to Octavia that Brenda received it as them complaining or making excuses. "I thought, she is not even taking in anything we say. She's listening, but she isn't really. I could tell that it wasn't changing her opinion or her perspective at all."

Octavia recalled, "The other thing that disturbed me, she wasn't even looking at me. She was talking about my program, and she was looking at my boss the whole time. I thought, *You're talking about my program, and I'm the one who runs it. You're not talking about people who are early career, no training at all. You hired competent, capable people for a reason.* So, there is a way that I feel like my personhood is not being respected, or I can't bring my full self in there somehow. When I had that insight about her, that was when I thought, *What if I pulled her hair?*"

This interaction with Brenda was not isolated. Not long after this meeting, Brenda took issue with Octavia's preparation of information for an internal audience. Brenda said, "This is unacceptable. This should never go out like this."

Octavia responded, "Really? This was an internal document to one of my colleagues just so she knows what projects our partners are working on. It's not going on our website. It's not going anywhere."

Octavia recalled, "In the moment, I ended up feeling like I'd had my hand slapped by her, and like we were not able to understand each other's perspective. It wasn't like I did not still have my perspective. It was just that there was no room for it within that interaction with her." As it became clear to Octavia that Brenda was not willing to consider another's perspective, Octavia's own capacity to inquire and take the perspective of another disappeared. First Octavia became defensive. Then she acquiesced.

Octavia lamented, "I just ended up explaining why things were that way. And saying, 'Now that I understand what you want, it's fine. I can update it. It is clear what you are requesting.'"

Yet, later, outside of the circumstance, outside of the grip, Octavia was able to step back and more objectively challenge some of Brenda's assumptions and perspectives. "If I'd had my full capacity, I would have wanted to offer an inquiry in that moment and also ask her to put more meat on the bones of her advocacy. *Why is this unacceptable?* Not to just take it as is." Octavia noted, "Reasonable people can disagree about whether or not something is acceptable. I would have wanted to take that larger perspective, to be able to balance between our two viewpoints, and not from a position of defensiveness. In my full capacity, I would have been able to defend my viewpoint, but from a space of, *Let's look at this. What's going on? Let's have a larger conversation about what's happening.*"

Octavia later realized that she didn't actually disagree with Brenda about certain things. "Nobody's going to argue that these were beautiful, polished videos. They weren't. I'm not stupid," Octavia noted. Octavia also came to understand that agreeing with Brenda, or not, wasn't the point. She conceded, "In fact, Brenda was not incorrect in some of the stuff she was saying. And also, it was not right, either, because it wasn't the full story. For me, it really was important to be able to have a more complex view of the situation; to be able to mediate between her very narrow, focused, and specific view of the situation."

Octavia knew she had the capacity to inquire into the complexity of a situation, to surface the different perspectives, but that ability was beyond her grasp in her interactions with Brenda. Advocacy closed the door on inquiry. Instead of opening up perspectives and possibilities, Octavia began to shut down in response to Brenda's unilateral approach.

Octavia recalled, "Our environment had been very free and creative. I didn't feel like I had to dot my I's and cross my T's. When Brenda came along and asserted herself in that way, I had this image of a dictator. Nobody likes people having power over them. But for me, that's a very particular trigger. It's something about a loss of freedom because I feel like somebody is trying to assert themselves onto me. That feels like an unsafe environment for me."

Suddenly, Octavia found herself in an environment that was not respectful, that didn't allow her full self to be present. She explained, "I feel like Brenda is controlling. The threat that I see from her is an environment where I feel trapped, or where I'm not going to be respected as a person and professional. I remember leaving the meeting thinking, *I can't stay here if I'm going to have to be under this.*"

Octavia started thinking it was time to find a new job at a new organization. She recalled, "I knew I was in a bad space when I had that thought."

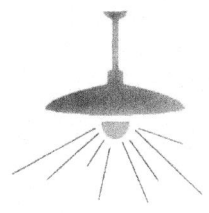

CHAPTER 4
GHOST LIGHT

You will come to see in the pages that follow that the "isolated stories" that Octavia and Robbin told were indeed stories that they, like Diego, had been rewriting. When we fall back, we tend to think of our experiences as solitary and unusual scenes in an otherwise pristine storyline. In fact, the characters that came on stage during the episodes of fallback that Diego, Robbin, and Octavia described were "the usual suspects," as Diego so aptly named them. They knew these characters well, though their inclination had been to keep them in the shadows, hidden in the darkness so that they and no one else would have to face them.

But if we take a cue from theater,[1] we discover that attempting to keep our unwanted parts of self locked in a darkened alley off the stage door only invites them to wreak havoc.

You see, in theaters around the world, a single light bulb is left burning on the stage whenever the theater is dark. It's called a ghost light. Theater lore tells us that the ghost light invites the ghosts that are said to inhabit all theaters to come onto the stage. It's a welcoming and an acknowledgement of the spirits that are part of every theater. Some say that if the light goes out, ghosts assume the theater is abandoned and cause mischief.

There's also a more practical reason for the presence of the ghost light on theater stages. If someone were to wander onto the stage when the theater is dark, they could easily go off the edge and into the orchestra pit. The ghost light is a safety measure. It helps guard against one falling in a pit.

Perhaps we should turn on the ghost light within self. Make it known that all spirits are welcome here. Invite them to show us their specialty, their range, to reveal their backstory. Welcome their characteristics that are shadowy and dark while also leaving open the possibility that they are not one-dimensional, that there is good within them, that a plot twist may be in the works—if we are willing to stick with the show.

In the chapters that follow, we will do just that. You will come to know your cast of characters, both the heroes and the villains. You'll explore the scenes of your life in which these characters are cast, identifying the cues that beckon them on stage. You'll learn when they serve the scene and when they don't. Having become familiar with the plot and the script of your play, you will act as director in the scenes of your life, casting the characters, designing the set, putting in place the props, and engaging in rehearsal. Interspersed in the chapters throughout, Robbin, Diego, Octavia, and I will serve as your guides as we notice, reflect upon, identify the triggers for, and recover and grow from our own fallback. And you will be invited to do the same.

To be clear, our goal is not to illuminate our fallback characters so we may once and for all banish them from the theater. You will never be rid of this piece of self. And you don't want to be. These characters that storm the stage, that go off script, are integral members of your cast. They have something important to teach you. They come prepared with lines that they have been trying to speak for some time. Our goal is to listen to them and to learn.

By undertaking this character study in the pages that follow, you will come to understand what this part of you is protecting in you, what it is that feels threatened when these characters come on the scene. You will have the opportunity to befriend them, to understand them, to form a different relationship to this part of you that you have attempted to keep hidden from self and from others. You will cast supporting actors that allow your fallback characters to take up their role in a more helpful manner. You will offer them lines that better convey your intentions and articulate how they are not being met in a given moment. You will increase your skill as playwright, acting coach, and director.

So let's resist the temptation to turn off the ghost light when the story itself gets too dark, lest those characters that reside within us assume that the playhouse of self has been abandoned and begin to cause mischief. Because they will. Actors live to be seen, to be acknowledged. Every single part of us, light and dark, does too. We can either set up the illumination and clear the way for the full ensemble to come on stage, or we can risk the characters wandering on stage in the darkness, stumbling off the edge and into a pit. It happens. Best to leave the light on for them.

After all, they're going to be an ever-present member of your cast for a while. They've signed a lock-tight contract. We would be well-served to get to know the full ensemble.

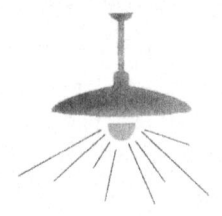

CHAPTER 5
NOTICING

At the beginning of the pandemic in March 2020, I was invited to speak on a newly created podcast, "Pandemic Companions," that executive coach Gideon Culman had envisioned to provide support and companionship through what many of us at the time thought would be a three-week lockdown to effectively "flatten the curve" of the novel coronavirus. As the whispers of what was to come became full-volume pronouncements from elected officials and the media, Gideon made the sojourn to the store to stock up on supplies, including what had suddenly become the scarce roll of toilet paper. He had been trying to quietly scoot past a woman in a grocery store aisle as she stood staring at the empty shelves in the refrigerated section when she spun around and snapped at him. He thought, *Ahh, this is fallback*, and quickly deduced we'd be seeing a lot more of it in the coming weeks of lockdown. Thus, Gideon's invitation to me to speak about fallback on his podcast.[1]

Many of us, like Gideon, could see fallback happening all around us *out there*. But before long, we couldn't help but begin to notice our own experiences of fallback. It turns out that lockdowns offer little space to hide from anyone in your household, including yourself.

Yet, fallback doesn't only happen in the time of pandemic, or unending episodes of systemic racial injustice, or election years, or any of the full-on shit show that made up the year 2020. 2020 was just the year we found it harder to deny the existence of a smaller self because, for many of us, the smaller self had stolen the show. I guess hindsight really is 2020.

Beginning to notice the times when we show up with less than our optimal developmental capacities is the first step in coming into relationship with our fallback.

Why Notice? Calling a Spade a Spade

When we are in fallback, it feels awful, constricting, and our thoughts go immediately to how we can break free. We often dismiss the way we show up in fallback. We say, "Well, that's just not me. This wasn't my fault," instead of asking what this fallback is trying to protect in us. "I did show up poorly or in a way that I wish I had not or that didn't meet my intentions. What's that about?"

Often, our most immediate reaction is to blame others. "It's your fault. You did me wrong." Eventually we realize that it's not them, or it is but only partially. And then comes the shame of *I got it wrong, again.* And that doesn't feel good either, so we try to push that away. Admittedly, in the present, it is often very hard for us to recognize and claim the parts of us that are smaller, scarier, more shadowy.

We have a notion that we are a consistent, enduring self that somehow remains whole and unbuffeted by the context around us. Our attention and our memories collude in this cover-up of who we really are by pushing down the ick and serving up the delights of self. That small self gets a sideways glance. "Ooh, who are you?" we ask with disdain as our scarier characters take over the scene. We pretend that we've never seen them before. As we shoo them off the stage, we likewise usher them out of our thoughts. But just because they've gone offstage does not mean that they are gone. And as long as we insist upon not acknowledging their role, they will continue to assert their presence.

Indeed, the recognition of self in fallback is *the move*. It's the step away from being fully in the grip. In some ways, you are still fully claimed by it, but there's a part of you that is observing the you that is fully claimed by it, maybe in the moment or maybe only after the fact. That noticing can be monumental. Monumental in its pain, because you see the damage to self, to others. But also monumental in recovery, and monumental in growth.

Through each of the experiences of fallback that Diego, Octavia, Robbin, and I recounted, there were different degrees of a niggling awareness that we were not showing up our best self. We were assailed, but not by some strange outside force. We were overtaken by a version of ourselves that may have felt jarring to ourselves and others in the moment but was not unknown.

If one's developmental center of gravity points to stability and steadiness, the experience of disequilibrium may be a clue that one has fallen off balance and into fallback. The research that has been conducted on fallback offers a glimpse into how this disequilibrium shows up in our experiences of fallback—in the behaviors, feelings, and bodily sensations that are present as well as those that are absent. Understanding these signs may allow us to notice ourselves in fallback more quickly.

Behavior

The participants in David McCallum's seminal research demonstrated the multitude of ways that fallback may show up in behavior that is out of alignment with one's normal way of being. In some of McCallum's participants, fallback presented as a subordination of one's self, one's needs and desires.[2] This manifested in a number of behaviors including "playing nice" and conforming to norms in order to accommodate and seek the approval of others.

We see an acquiescence to norms playing out with Octavia, who while in the grip of fallback in her interactions with Brenda was unable to do the thing that she knew she otherwise could—inquire into Brenda's perspective and articulate her own in a way that sought to bridge understanding. Instead, though Octavia didn't share the director's perspective, she began to question herself. In the moment, she capitulated to Brenda's expectations, as uninformed by context as Octavia thought they were.

McCallum also noted a regression to childhood tendencies and patterns as a behavior in fallback. When Brenda criticized Octavia's discernment, Octavia felt like she just had to take it. "Yes, it is unacceptable. Bad girl! You should do this differently." Though she didn't act on it, Octavia also had a desire to pull Brenda's hair, an inclination reminiscent of Octavia's elementary school days.

Diego, too, reverted to the patterns of his youth. In his early twenties, Diego was driven to be the winner. This younger aspect of Diego stormed the stage, subsuming his capacity to connect to Kyra's perspective. He became curt, impatient, speaking in shorter sentences, interrupting, and raising his voice. Diego could only see black-and-white, win or lose. This competitive self-focus that characterized Diego's behavior is another of the fallback orientations found in McCallum's research.

McCallum also observed fight, flight, and freeze orientations in his participants. Diego's primitive *fight* instinct emerged in his fallback with Kyra as he "went for the kill" in protection of all of the aspects of self he felt slipping away. Self-orientation took over as he sought to take control and win. Diego described tumbling through a wormhole to more primal and instinctive parts of self, those that lurk in the shadow, that, in fact, are his shadow. Indeed, behaviors in fallback can be primal and are often experienced and viewed as "behaving badly" and acting impulsively out of anger and hurt.[3]

Projecting onto and blaming others were also frequently noted fallback behaviors in McCallum's study that may fall into the fight domain. During the first weeks of the pandemic, Robbin made his children, his wife, and his predatory landlord responsible for his angst, and his response was to roar.

Yet Octavia's orientation in her fallback was to bolt. When Octavia felt her autonomy and sense of fairness threatened by Brenda, she wanted to *flee* and began looking for the first escape hatch.

Others in McCallum's study experienced apathy, felt disoriented, lost their sense of agency, and in some cases shut down completely, disconnected both from self and others. Throughout 2020, Robbin would *freeze*, sinking into the depths of his despair, unable to act at all.

McCallum would later add to the list of fallback behaviors that he identified during his study an unwillingness to show vulnerability, a grasping for control, and acting and speaking from the head rather than integrating the wisdom of the physical and emotional selves.[4]

During my research with the thought leaders in the field, Torbert, Berger, and Kegan pointed to many of the same behaviors indicating disequilibrium in fallback that McCallum had identified in his study. In addition, Torbert identified actions and behaviors associated with fallback, including sleeping to avoid further fallback behaviors, behaving unilaterally, privileging one's own experience over that of others, becoming self-protective and minimizing risk, and becoming less conversational and less perception-testing.[5]

Becoming aware of the ways we show up when we don't have access to our full capacities becomes a helpful tool for noticing when we have fallen back. We start to know what to look for. We can spot it on the scene more quickly. When we are in fallback, we can cultivate the capacity to notice that the characters that are taking their marks on the stage are different from those who are generally (or perhaps the more accurate word is *optimally*) cast in the scenes of our lives. Holding how we are behaving up against how we intend to be can also help us notice that we are in fallback.

But important clues are available not only by noticing what is present but also what is missing.

Loss

Loss is pervasive in fallback. When we are in fallback, we experience a loss of perspective, of full capacities to be bigger, of options, of language and distinction. Berger described the experience of fallback as feeling self slipping back and becoming constrained, smaller, and unable to feel into one's fullness. The field shrinks, certainty solidifies. She noted that fallback occurs when one's perspective narrows and one can contain only one idea for a time; when there is a loss of something that you would otherwise have access to. It is fallback if an earlier thought, feeling, or action exists in the absence of other thoughts, feelings, actions. In other words, it's fallback if the earlier meaning you make is in isolation, if you lose the capacity to make meaning from your biggest self.[6]

Torbert's personal experience of fallback is marked by an inability to connect to richness and his own vital core. He described falling back as a flattened world experience, a re-experiencing characterized by past archetypes along a familiar downward tunnel, during which he loses the capacity for choice in action. McCallum observed a loss of appreciation for the richness and complexity of the human experience in fallback.[7]

Loss echoed through Robbin's, Diego's, and Octavia's experiences, as well. Robbin lost his connection to the living beings outside of himself. He observed, "It feels like me against the world. Me against my wife. Me against my kids. And when you have these chubby-cheeked little beings who look up to you as a hero, and you're meeting them with me against them, it's heartbreaking."

Robbin also lost spaciousness. "I recognized who I had known myself to be, but I had no access to him, and I was frustrated about that," recalled Robbin. "I felt smaller than my normal self, like I was trapped inside of behavior that I'm used to judging as shitty but didn't seem able to not engage in it at that moment, even if I thought that there was some way to not engage in it. It's a trapped-ness."

As the doors to the rooms of his developmental house slammed shut around him, Diego lost his capacity to navigate complexity. Diego described the closing off of other perspectives, the closing down of options, as being thrown into a wormhole. Diego recalled, "It was a confusion that was totally terrifying, because I was prisoner to it, totally enmeshed in it." Diego also lost access to the person he thought he was, the values he had espoused.

Octavia, while able to observe herself in the moment, was unable to balance between her perspective and Brenda's, and lost the capacity to inquire and act in a way that she could have when she was outside of the grip of fallback. Octavia observed, "I had a moment in one of the meetings where I could recognize that there was a shift. On one hand, I was myself. I did have some of my capacity. And I could see myself going back and forth between a meta-view and this under-attack view or experience." Yet, even as she was able to observe it, Octavia was not able to shift the dynamic or behave differently. She said, "That was a big part of the fallback experience, because I was not able to fully hold my own perspective in that moment or balance between her perspective and my perspective." This not being able to hold both perspectives, something that Octavia is generally capable of, led to feelings of shame and incompetence.

Tapping into our cognitive knowing can provide clues that we are in fallback. Yet we may also benefit from taking a broader view beyond the chatter of the brain in fallback as we cultivate our awareness. When anxieties arise, when we feel ourselves shrinking, we can connect to the physical sensations and step away from thinking.

Bodily Sensations

Our bodily sensations can provide a visceral indication that we are sliding into the abyss of our smaller selves. During his experience of fallback with Kyra, Diego felt the heat rising in his chest, his muscles tensed. In the midst of her interactions with Brenda, Octavia felt her heart rate go up. "I could tell I was feeling under attack, or feeling defensive," Octavia recalled. Noticing what is happening to our breath, our heartbeat, our skin, our muscles, our bones, our throat, can signal when our operating system is on alert, experiencing attack.

It's damn hard to deny that the wheels have fallen off the wagon when the body is enacting its equivalent to red lights blinking, alarms blaring, and steam escaping. Yet we often push the gift of this clue to notice aside. We ignore the warning it provides to take note and then attempt to get ourselves back online, or to slowly and calmly exit the building until the threat has been assessed and it's safe to re-enter. Instead, we get swept up in the riptide, disoriented in the surf.

Though our bodies sustain life, we sometimes feel detached from them or fight against the wisdom they offer. Yet connecting to our bodily sensations can be a powerful tool for noticing fallback in its unfolding. The goal is to access all sources of information and tools for noticing and reframing without judgment—the mind, heart, and body.

Torbert suggested that our awareness of the body and the mind can be cultivated through the process of meditation. He explained, "Mindfulness and meditation can be tools if the effort is carried out with sufficient instruction so that one can begin to separate thinking from mindfulness. It's not something that happens in a finished way, once and for all, but is an actual process. And as you're in the situation, you're in awareness that different things transform, in Kegan's terms, from subject to object within you.[8] It's the process of trying to become connected to a trans-cognitive awareness in the moment, which in my teaching meant going down into the body first, rather than up into the clouds, and having a mindfulness that encompasses one's body, one's feelings and one's thoughts. And that slips away very quickly. Almost immediately it turns into mere thought about the idea of mindfulness. So, it's no simple discipline."[9]

When we fall back, we are *unconsciously* acting, feeling, making meaning from a developmental space that is earlier than that to which we generally have access. For that moment—be that an actual moment, or five, or three hours, or thirty days—we have lost access to the choices we have available when at our fuller capacity. Yet when we can name the behaviors that manifest in our fallback, when we can identify what is lost in those moments, when we pay attention to the bodily sensations that indicate we may be tunneling down into a smaller version of ourselves, we are more apt to notice.

I believe noticing is the linchpin in all of this. Notice and name, and notice and inquire, and notice and refine. It is in the noticing that we come into a more honest, authentic relationship with the many versions of us that come into the scenes of our lives in the course of a day. While this kind of encompassing consciousness of self from moment to moment is a capacity that is more readily available as one moves further along the developmental spectrum, we may be able to build the muscle of awareness through practice at any stage.

CHAPTER 6
VALERIE NOTICING

On the occasion of my would-be-joyful-memory-making breakfast outing with my small children becoming seared into my memory for all the wrong reasons, there were many clues in my behavior that a smaller version of self had taken over. I could feel it building inside of me—the hyperalertness as I looked for my children to make the wrong move, the lack of flexibility in the rules for how we behave in public.

I could find no compassion for my children or for the restaurant employees, who I blamed for the delays. I was convinced that I was the victim, and the world was conspiring against me. Why was it taking so long for us to get our food? Where was the waitstaff? Why couldn't my children just sit still, behave, and follow the script I had written for them?

In that restaurant, this blame turned into anger toward everyone in that room, and I wanted to lash out. I was curt and gruff and jolting. I wanted the kids to know that I was unhappy and that they were the reason. When I fall back, often my first reaction is to take it out on those I feel are causing me to be smaller. I have a name for this character: Punitive One.

My physical body offered signs that I was plummeting down, as well. When I am in fallback, my attention sweeps inward and down to a tiny crevice of my brain tissue where it feels trapped. My muscles tense and my jaw bones grind together. My eyes narrow and my body feels propelled forward. My amygdala is on high alert, and it is communicating to my body to be at the ready. Heat rushes through my hands, my belly, my heart, up to the roots of my hair. My heartbeat has ramped up its rhythm and its intensity. Perhaps this accounts for the pull, the ache that I feel in my chest and my throat. The yelling always catches in my throat, causing me to cough. Attempting to clear it; to expel the it out of me. This is a signal. Pay attention, Val. You're spiraling. Noted. Sometimes heeded. Often not.

In my experience with my children, I could see it all happening, but I had lost capacity to show up differently. I was navigating a well-worn path of smallness. I could see that there were other actions I needed to take, yet I couldn't access them. I watched myself in disgust, unable to turn it around. I knew I needed to breathe. Not the shallow, perfunctory breaths that fueled my jerkiness, but the deep, long, nourishing breaths that both make and clear space. But I couldn't breathe.

My first instinct was to lash out. My second was to flee. Though not just to flee from those who I blamed—my children, the waitstaff. I wanted to escape from myself...this smaller self that was in no way a reflection of my intentions but from which I was unable to break free.

As anger rose within me, sadness settled like a fog. I needed out of this situation that I had created that clearly was not going the way I had envisioned.

While the signals to notice that I was in fallback were plentiful within me in the moment—in my body, in my behaviors, in the recognition of the capacities that I was missing—there were also clues in my external environment that this was a circumstance ripe for the wheels coming off the wagon. Paying attention to the setting, the props and costumes, and the characters of the other actors on the scene would have provided additional data that, if heeded, may have helped me change course and avert the fallback firestorm.

I knew that I wasn't in top form. In the months prior, I had been tasked with a project at work that was a complete departure from what I had been hired to do, had pulled me away from the soul-feeding aspects of my job, and had required me to cancel time off with my family and time that I had anticipated devoting to researching and writing this book. I had not been sleeping well. I was not showing up well to much in my life. I was not in a good place.

My kiddos were also not primed for a successful outing in public. I knew that they had been awake since before 5 a.m. They'd been away from their own home, their own stuff, their own people. Much as they know Leah well and adore her, there's also a degree of emotional stress that comes from being in a place that is not home, a stress that without fail gets expressed during the reintegration with the familiar.

We often have a script playing in our head that we do not make explicit to the outside world or even to ourselves. We have expectations for particular scenes. And we are invested in those storylines playing out in the way we envision.

After not having spent much time with the kids, my expectations were high for what this breakfast would accomplish: reconnection, the stuff that memories are made of, enough to sustain us through my coming days away. Yet, these expectations for the scenes of our lives and the way we will show up in them frequently get us in trouble. And they land us in even deeper water when we don't acknowledge their presence.

I should have read the program before walking into the performance. If I had done so I could have noticed the storyline that I had running. I had a lot loaded up in this one experience with my children. My expectations were high and unyielding. I was going to control my way into success. The problem was, there was so much outside of my control: my children's behavior, the waitstaff's efficiency, access to my own capacities that were increasingly becoming locked behind the doors in my developmental house.

I could also have connected to my own intentions for this performance. I lost touch with what lived within me, and my children, and the struggles and triumphs of every other person surrounding us that day. My attention went inward and down to a narrow and flat existence. All else was blurred and superfluous. Yet, that "all else" is the thing that truly mattered and the underlying reason for my even having persisted in the event. And in that moment, it was all lost.

CHAPTER 7
YOUR TURN TO NOTICE

When we are just beginning to cultivate an awareness of the true self as we are, it is difficult to do so in the moment. It takes practice to begin to notice how we are showing up in the scenes of our life. As we are starting out, our practice may take the form of noticing ourselves *after the fact*, in retrospect.

Freewriting is a tool that has been powerful in my own discovery of self, a discovery of a self that is nowhere near as consistent as I like to imagine it to be. There are aspects of self we keep in the shadows in hopes that we and others might forget that those parts exist. Freewriting—putting fingers to keys, or pencil to paper, and just letting your unconscious knowing flow without regard for spelling, grammar, or organization, or even a goal of it making sense—coaxes out the hidden, multiple aspects of self.

Exercise

Let's begin to feel into the contours of the scenes of our lives and a recognition of ourselves in these. Reflect on the unfolding story of your life over the past year. Play back the video reel of what happened, paying special attention to yourself on the "screen."

Identify a specific moment of grace. A moment when you were in flow, in alignment with how you wish to see yourself in the world, in alignment with who you wish to be. As you watch the playback, how would you describe yourself in that moment? What was alive for you? What were you doing? Feeling? Thinking? How were you behaving? What felt good?

Set a timer for five minutes and just let the answers to these questions flow through your fingertips onto the keyboard or through your pencil onto paper.

Now, as you watch the playback, identify a specific moment of fallback. A moment when you felt yourself shrinking; your options for showing up, limited; your normal capacities, gone. Perhaps it was an experience of feeling out of sync with yourself, with those around you. Maybe it felt like a departure from whom you wish to be seen as, whom you wish to be. From this detached viewer perspective, how would you describe yourself in that moment? What was alive for you? What were you doing? What thoughts were going through your mind? What did that feel like?

Again, set a timer for five minutes and allow your inner knowing to come forth through freewriting.

There will be some characters that you are proud to claim in your cast, that you wish everyone who knows you to see. And you will have other characters that you wish you could deny. These are not the ones you want to be known for, though there is probably an aspect of them that we can and likely have put a positive spin on. But here we are exploring our fallback characters, the ones that take us back into our smaller self, the ones that don't allow us to meet our intentions.

What is the gap there, between intentions and reality? And what is your felt experience of showing up in that gap? Set your timer for three minutes and write about this.

Hold onto this writing. You will use it again as you move through the "Your Turn" chapters throughout this book.

CHAPTER 8
REFLECTING

Noticing that we are in the smaller confines of our developmental house is monumental in our coming to know the fullness of self. But noticing in isolation does not lead to growth. Poking around in the drawers and closets of these constrained spaces is necessary if we aspire to maximize and stretch into our full being. And in this probing of our fallback, we will inevitably find the gap between the self we believe we are and aspire to be, and the way we are actually showing up in the world.

Stage development theory, no matter the nuanced approach, posits that we contain all of ourselves, including the smallest aspect. Each level is transcended and included, not destroyed. Given that all levels are contained within us, we must have the ability to slip into or access earlier stages. It is our ability and willingness to reflect on those forays into our less complex self, the rooms with fewer tools and options, that allows us to learn from our fallback and transform our relationship with the many parts of self that are us. This ability and willingness increases as we unlock the rooms in our developmental house.

Unlocking the Rooms in Our Developmental House

In the process of development, we take those things we have been subject to—parts of self and the world we live in, things that we had not been able to see before because there was no separation between us and them—and we gradually, over time and with much effort and commitment, separate them out from the self. This process is referred to as taking what we are subject to and making it object. In taking a thing as object we are able to hold it—a value, a belief, an aspect of our identity or ego, an institution—apart from us in order to examine it and question it. In so doing, we increase our capacity to hold complexity.[1]

One of the capacities that becomes increasingly available as we unlock more rooms in our developmental house is our ability and willingness to take more things as object, to notice more, to have an awareness of the kind of human we wish to be in this world and to hold that up against the way we actually are from day to day, moment to moment. More complex developmental capacity allows us to examine and probe aspects of self that are not part of our idealized version. The whole of us does not feel quite as at stake should these parts of us be exposed…to self and to others.

During my earlier research on fallback with the key thinkers, both Torbert and McCallum noted that individuals at later action logics[2] or stages of complexity have access to an "encompassing consciousness" that more frequently notices fallback and recovers from it—access that those who make meaning at the conventional action logics do not tend to possess. Torbert observed that this ever-increasing awareness leads to a more frequent noticing of the incongruities in one's life and actions.[3]

McCallum recalled from his own research, "Those with later-stage capacity had a quicker belay of their regression. They also had a much wider repertoire of inner resources that they could draw upon to stop the fallback, to, in a sense, make sense. And not just cope, but actually adapt in that moment in a way that was potentially timely and transforming. For instance, in the midst of action to consider, *what would I really want to do in this situation?* Or, *let me just take a moment and breathe.* Or, *oh my gosh, this person is projecting something on me, and I am not going to buy into it.* Those were amazing kinds of moves. Folks in the earlier stages had a much harder time noticing the fallback and taking that kind of nuanced perspective on it."[4]

To be sure, the developmental capacities at later stages do not solve all of life's problems, do not make individuals better or smarter or more ethically sound, and they do not make us immune to falling back, but they do allow us to notice our fallback more frequently and closer to the event. Individuals at later stages have greater capacity to reflect on their fallback without it feeling like complete obliteration of self. And they are more capable of seeing a self that is not enduring and constant, of coming to know and accept the more shadowy characters that make up one's self, and of imagining more possibilities for showing up differently. While development may not offer the stairway to heaven that people idealize, it does offer us more enhanced tools and capacities to tap into as we face into the complexity of what it is to be human, that allow us to cultivate our relationship to our fallback.

Paradoxically, when we build the muscle of noticing and reflecting, our experience of being locked out of the rooms of our developmental house in fallback may ultimately lead to the opening up of new rooms. The abrupt tumbling that often marks fallback shines a spotlight on that which we have been subject to, unable to see. It puts what had been hidden to us center stage to be examined, probed, inquired into. Engaging in reflection to understand our fallback—how it presents, what's at stake—leads to the ability to use it and work with it differently. In this process of illumination, what was once subject becomes object, explicit, known, seen, acknowledged. And this is how development happens.

Minding the Gap

We likely are not accustomed to paying attention in the moment to the way we are showing up in the world and differentiating it from the way we claim to be. Minding the gap between these two is a practice that can help us build our awareness of the many parts of self that show up in the scenes of our lives and is a key part of reflection.

Our first step may be reflection on action.[5] We fall back and perhaps we are so triggered or so caught up that we don't even see it happening in the moment. The awareness is only available to us once we are out of the grip. In the aftermath, we shake our heads in disappointment at ourselves and think, *Damn, I really messed that up.*

Becoming clear about what our intentions are for a scene, in our relationships with others and ourselves, and building our awareness of what we look and feel like at our best can help us become aware when we have strayed from those intentions, from the bigger version of self.

Our narrative of self offers a touchstone against which to hold up our current behavior or meaning-making, offering a comparison of both points, the ideal and the gap. In order to understand, accept, and grow, we must mind the gap with tolerance and forgiveness, recognizing that these aspects of self that we desperately want to reject and deny are key parts of who we are.

Fallback is an integral piece of what makes you whole. It's not always positive, and it doesn't always feel good. However, primal emotions and experiences are a signal that something important is going on, providing a wake-up call that may lead us to our bigger self. There's something about being confronted with the data in the moment that makes it less easy to run from or deny. We need to pay attention rather than reject the experience.

Jennifer Garvey Berger noted, "It is normal that we dip into these places. It's not wrong or bad. It feels like what it is to be alive...to stretch into the full range of our humanness, the full range of our development, and to sometimes be caught in one eddy before we can break free. It has seemed to me that there are always important things to learn in the eddy. There is always something in that swirl that's going to help me or others, even if it just helps me be more compassionate with other people who are in that thrashing space. There's always something."[6]

Over time, as we purposefully pay attention to our episodes of fallback by engaging in the practice of reflection on action, after the fact, we can develop a capacity for reflection in action.[7] Reflection in action is a watching awareness *in the moment*. We may not have the capacity to change our behavior, thoughts, or feelings at the time of fallback. No other options may exist. But we are able to witness the fullness of our self as our fallback is unfolding.

Octavia could see that she did not have her full capacities in the moment of her interactions with Brenda. She could watch herself showing up more constricted, but she was powerless to access different options at that time. Yet, later, outside of the circumstance, outside of the grip, Octavia was able to step back and more objectively challenge some of Brenda's assumptions and perspectives and notice the smaller space within herself from which she responded.

Octavia recalled, "I did a lot of reflection around it when I was out of the situation and could take a larger view that I was not able to take in the moment. I realized that it's fine for her to have her perspective. Brenda's perspective is just one perspective among many, and it's not necessarily *the* perspective, even if she is our division director. I got caught up in that whole needing to look competent."

Reflection in action is a monumental step in our coming into different relationship with our fallback because we are building the reflexive muscle to witness ourselves as we fall back and to take note of the confluence of factors swirling around and within us. This gives us data that we can probe, that we can work with to anticipate who might come on the stage and why in our future scenes and what our options for movement and scripting may be.[8]

Octavia noted, "An important thing for me is to be able to recognize sooner what these patterns are, to be able to see what's going on. Because, before, I just couldn't. I'd be like, *Shit! I'm in it! And I don't even realize!* I was still subject to it. And now I can see it. And I can even get out of it a little bit quicker." Over time and with practice and ongoing reflection, Octavia was able to develop a watching awareness of self in the moment of fallback.

Robbin, too, was able to observe the fallback, but unable to access options to shift directions in the moment. Robbin's awareness of what was happening when his daughter punched him spanned two levels. "There was the one level at which I just completely got triggered by Elsa punching me, and I lost my shit," Robbin explained. "But there was the other, longer-term level that I could see but didn't really have access to operating from. I shouldn't be doing this. I should be calm. I don't know how this is going to further erode the environment that we're living in right now. But I wasn't exhibiting observable behaviors from that place," Robbin continued. "And at the level of observable behavior was, *My physical safety is at risk.*"

While Robbin was unable to change his behaviors in the moment of fallback, he was able to connect to an incredibly valuable piece of information—to notice what felt at risk to him. Becoming aware of what feels threatened in our experiences of fallback can profoundly reshape our relationship to the parts of self that we wish to banish. We come to see these characters that often show up in the scenes of our fallback not as evil villains but as valiant protectors, bumbling and ill-scripted as they may be. When we can appreciate that they are here to protect us, we are more inclined to open ourselves up to notice and reflect on them.

Reflecting on our fallback offers us glimpses of our fallback tendencies, allows us to identify our characters and gain insight into what they are protecting and what scenes beckon them, and provides clues to notice, arrest, and recover from our fallback sooner. Reflection on fallback allows us to be more intentional about how we are showing up to the scenes of our lives and to notice when our actions are not aligned with our intentions.

Our capacity to change our automatic responses and to make a different choice in the moment of fallback can be expanded through paying attention as a practice. Brain scientists David Rock and Jeffrey Schwartz point to awareness as a critical component in changing the structure of the brain. They note, "At a moment of insight, a complex set of new connections is being created. These connections have the potential to enhance our mental resources and overcome the brain's resistance to change. But to achieve this result, in the brain's limited working memory, we need to make a deliberate effort to hardwire an insight by paying it repeated attention."[9]

We pay the insights—the information that fallback offers us—repeated attention by noticing our fallbacks and steadfastly reflecting on them. This is aided when we remain present in these moments of learning rather than withdrawing from the situation and allowing the established patterns of our brain to take over.[10] As we come to a more robust understanding in relationship to our fallback, as we connect to our intentions, and as we purposefully employ tools to help us recover, we engrain patterns in the brain that allow new neuropathways to be formed.

Whether while in the grip of fallback or after it has passed, noticing that we are without our options, tools, perspectives—the stuff in the locked rooms within our developmental house—is a skill we can begin to cultivate. Eventually, we can develop the capacity to be simultaneously present to what is happening in the moment and halt the action or give ourselves different direction. We might still fall into the orchestra pit but recover more quickly. Or sometimes we are able to catch ourselves as we are stumbling, to make a different choice and to recover in real time.

This process may take time and practice to cultivate. And in the beginning, we may only notice the blockbuster performances of our smaller self, not the bit roles that they are regularly cast in.

Robbin could not help but notice that a smaller version of himself was on the scene when his fallback reached epic proportions, but he struggled to take note of the less-intense experiences of showing up a more constricted version of himself. However, with time and through the practice of reflection, Robbin began to cultivate a capacity for noticing the little moments of fallback that he had previously swept under the rug. He observed, "Increasingly, I've been noticing my fallback characters showing up not at full volume, but maybe two or three on a ten scale. And mind you, until our deep dive, I'd really only noticed the characters when they were going full throttle."

Robbin mused, "It's enlightening to map these episodes we've been exploring onto phenomena that I've long identified, but just seemed random. And these characters only seemed to come into view when they were strutting across the stage, as opposed to noticing the glimpses of them always being there in the wings." One of the benefits of coming to know our characters is that we are able to pay attention to their more subtle insertions, not just the extreme.

The gift of fallback and the noticing of and reflecting upon it is that we are able to see our full ensemble including those who had perhaps been pulling the strings from behind the set because they weren't invited into full view. We are able to catch glimpses of the characters that are likely to take the stage, understand what feels threatened, and discover epiphanies about what is still alive in us that needs tending. We are offered a pause, fleeting as it may be, particularly as we are just beginning to cultivate this capacity for awareness, to connect to our intentions for our self, for our relationships. And we can see other options.

An awareness of the true self as we are, rather than the stories we tell ourselves or who we desire to be, is perhaps the most important step in our recovery from fallback. Taking a deep breath, connecting with spirit, becoming curious, and fighting through the shame and guilt of fallback allows us to take a perspective that may allow us to learn and grow in relationship to the many characters that comprise our ensemble of self.

CHAPTER 9
DIEGO REFLECTING

As humans, we tend to believe that we are one person, one self, consistent and enduring. We often have a hard time accepting and claiming the multiplicity of ways that we show up in the world and in relationship. Because in order to do so, we must endure great loss. We must relinquish a sense of self, of identity, of who we have known ourselves to be. When we are in fallback, we want to disown this smaller, uglier version of the self that is strutting across the stage of our lives.

The characters that stormed the stage in Diego's fallback with Kyra had been cast in other scenes of his life. Yet not until now was he willing to acknowledge their presence. Diego explained, "Because my relationship with Kyra was so important to me, the wake-up call was much stronger. Had it happened with someone I didn't care for, I could have ignored it. In fact, I had been ignoring it. In the process of reflection, I revisited four or five things that had happened in the last ten years that were fallback to the same place. I hadn't done the full exploration. I had just left them aside, and then went forward, and fell back again, and left them aside." Though this experience of fallback with Kyra felt novel and raw and awful, Diego would come to see with reflection that it was a persistent story in his life connected to loss of control and a desire to be seen in a certain way.

In the days and weeks that followed what Diego would come to refer to as "the breaking," when he demanded an all-or-nothing response to the future of their relationship and Kyra did not comply, Diego's reflection on his fallback experience came in the form of letters to Kyra. As Diego shined the ghost light on himself, he went through several steps in the process.

First, Diego began to identify what felt threatened in his fallback. At risk was the dream of a life with Kyra and the professional and romantic dimensions that comprised it. He was also overwhelmed by fear: fear of loneliness in old age, fear of not being in control, fear of not winning. Diego lashed out, determined at least to get even if he was not going to win.

Then came the confusion. As Diego reflected on his experience of fallback, he felt as though he had lost himself, that he didn't know who he was any longer. Diego wrote to Kyra, "I used to think that I was true to myself. I do not know what this means any longer because I have lost a sense of who I am. I feel broken in pieces, blown in the air, buffeted by a hurricane, no force putting the pieces back together and no safe place to touch ground again. The most potent factor behind the explosion is the suite of contradictions that the last week has uncovered. I believe that I am honest, yet I lie tactically. I make promises, and I break them without owning up. I am loving, and I am hard-hearted, if not cruel at times. I am devoted to the people I love, and yet I'm self-oriented and self-protective. I'm inspired by big ideas and thrill seeking, and I seek safety in matters that are trivial. I do not know how to hold polarities in difficult circumstances—being honest with Ellie and not hurting her. In short, I see myself as having always behaved in more tactical and more manipulative ways than I have ever been comfortable admitting to myself. I have lost myself and my inner compass, and I am disoriented. I have never felt so broken. I have never been brought face-to-face with my self-deceit and my contradictions. I have never disliked myself as much as I do now."

Diego was bewildered as he tried to make sense of himself as a complex being with many different and sometimes contradictory aspects of self, some that departed vastly from the person he knew himself to be. Diego had a sense of himself as loving and kind, as someone who was able to hold complexity and nuance, and who, when needed, could be a decisive actor. And in those moments with Kyra, the doors to those rooms in his developmental house slammed shut, leaving him with a much more constrained floor plan of self to navigate, one he couldn't locate himself within. He described himself as prisoner to the confusion, and he was terrified by it.

To be sure, this was not the first time Diego had found himself in these cramped rooms. But in the past, once he was able to get out, he secured caution tape to the doorways and vowed never to return. Until he did, again and again. But this time the stakes were too high to leave the rooms of self unexamined. Because what was at risk—a relationship with Kyra—was so incredibly important to him, Diego got curious about all of the parts of himself that had come on the scene of his fallback; curious about who and what would come next.

Diego wrote, "Am I happy that this is happening to me? Part of me hates it, and another part of me is fascinated. The latter part is gaining ground fast. The struggle is tragically painful, as tragic as any hero's journey. I sense that surrender will soon be inevitable. I have to go through the pain to find myself again. I want to face my self-recrimination, my self-disappointment, my self-loathing. The more I deconstruct, the faster this liminal space will spit me out on the other shore. Who will I be? Will I cohere again around a life that is itself congruent? Will I be as lovable to you as I once was? Will I have lost everything in a battle to find myself? Is my worst fear the price I pay to grow?"

With reflection over time, Diego could begin to understand and own these smaller aspects of himself. Diego wrote to Kyra, "There is in me a developmental wormhole. And in extreme circumstances it sends me tumbling down into less complex parts of myself that are stuck in earlier ways of making sense of myself and the world around me. When I'm thrown there, self-orientation takes hold, and I revert instinctively to using unilateral forms of power—logistical power and sometimes coercive and charming power. In that place, I lose perspective, I see no options, I find it impossible to see where the other person is coming from, impossible to find a handle back into my bigger self. The tiger turns into a ruthless wolverine that goes for the kill instinctively."

As Diego continued to ruminate on his experience of fallback, the details in his view on himself became clearer, though much more complex. Eleven days after "the breaking" with Kyra, Diego wrote, "The thread that has been floating in my mind is about generosity and self-orientation. I have been recalling all of the ways in which I am selflessly generous. I pass on loads of work to others without asking for anything else in return. If someone is asleep, I will go out of my way not to turn the lights on when I go about what I need to do. I give a lot of my time to help others figure out their lives. I rarely allow someone to take a restaurant bill. And yet at the very core of me is this useless force that will protect tight boundaries around my selfish needs and desires. And there is this wormhole tunneling process triggered by threats to my compulsive needs to be in control and to win. I am craving a way of introducing more softness, more agility, as I navigate this as a continuum, not as a snapping thing. I sense it is possible, but for now, it has been elusive."

Through Diego's recounting of his fallback with Kyra, we can see the intensity of the emotions in the moment. In the days and weeks that followed, we see unfold the confusion and shame and eventually the hints at a new and more complete understanding of self than existed before, a more honest relationship with the full range of self. In time, Diego began to come to terms with the dichotomy of himself. His confusion turned to acceptance.

Diego could see that he was not *this* or *that*—selfish and controlling *or* generous. He began to see that he is this *and* that—selfish and controlling *and* generous. He is all of these things. He is light and shadow. He is big and small. He began to see that there were other possibilities for how he could show up without being forced to an extreme, as had been his pattern. He just wasn't sure yet how to enact those possibilities. Yet in the naming, in the honest reckoning with the fullness of himself, the fallback and the characters that it beckoned onto the scene began to loosen their grip.

Self-reflection is one tool that aids in our making sense of our fallback. Reflection from others, both to recall the person we have been and to reveal the person we are becoming, is a significant supporting factor in revealing the gap between our espoused ways of being and who we actually are. Accompaniment by others serves as an anchor in our construction of self and is pivotal to our meaning-making and growth.

Diego engaged doggedly through his incoherence and confusion in coming to know himself anew and more honestly in the days and weeks following his fallback. And he wasn't alone. Kyra accompanied him in his recognition, reflecting who he was in fallback to him and carefully charging him to examine what was happening. She held him accountable and also offered acceptance by showing Diego the beauty in these parts of self that Diego could, for a time, only see as hideous. Diego recalled, "Kyra helped me see how those pieces of myself that I was self-loathing were actually essential parts of myself that were important and attractive and effective in the world."

What we can come to realize, as Diego did with time and reflection within self and with others, is that this, too, is me. And it's not going anywhere. Instead of rejecting these parts of self that feel smaller, shameful, and unworthy, we can approach them with curiosity and willingness to receive the lesson they are there to teach us. We can grow in relationship to our fallen back characters without rejecting what they represent.

As Diego wrote to Kyra, the characters who were present during his fallback spilled onto the page.

The Wolverine–"I am loving, and I am hard-hearted, if not cruel at times."

The Shamed Quitter–"I am devoted to the people I love, and yet I'm self-oriented and self-protective."

The Dreamer–"I'm inspired by big ideas and thrill seeking…"

The Cautious Ditherer–"…and I seek safety in matters that are trivial."

Over time, Diego identified these characters who were on stage in the fallback episode with Kyra, and several other characters in the events leading up to it that contributed to the drama. Still others would play integral supporting actor roles that were so engrained that Diego would not come to identify their presence on the stage until years later, though they had been there all along.

Diego would eventually invite each of these characters into the theater, onto the stage to be illuminated by the ghost light. He would come to know them intimately, to understand when they were written into the script, what cues brought them onto the stage, which costars they were cast alongside, and what role they served. The fallback scene that Diego described with Kyra was part of a larger act. Let us come to know the fuller story.

Backstory

Ellie was Diego's second wife. His first marriage had been unhealthy from the start and lasted for ten years before it became no longer tenable. Diego was bruised and confused following his divorce from his first wife, and he blamed himself for not understanding how to be in a marriage, how to build a family that could thrive.

Then he met Ellie. Ellie was raised in a healthy family, one which she was intent on reproducing. She had a clear set of principles and values about what family should be. Diego was enthralled by Ellie and her family and who she promised to be as a partner in life. He bought into that story and set out to win the part of Ellie's spouse.

Ellie and her family were less convinced of Diego's merits. Diego recalled, "Ellie was super concerned that because I had divorced once, I would be likely to divorce another time, and her parents were of the same mind. And so I constructed this persona, this character that was essentially the perfect partner, the perfect husband, the perfect dependable person: does the dishes, looks after himself and Ellie, and had all the makings of a good father." Diego polished the character and sold the role well enough for Ellie to acquiesce. It would be thirty years after the creation of this character that Diego would recognize the role that he had played in the scenes of his marriage and his difficulty in leaving it and give him a name: *P3– Picture Perfect Partner*.

Diego bought in fully to the promise of a marriage much different from his first, swallowing whole Ellie's values about what was right and true in a family. Diego remembered, "In my marriage with Ellie and in my parenthood, my sense of what was right and wrong was completely subsumed in the values that I had taken from her. My sense of fatherhood was fused with my sense of marriage. My relationship with my children was playful and protective. But it was very much, *I'm a parent, you're a child. I'm part of this marriage, and the relationship is defined by that. It's not defined by who I am as a person, or who you are as a person. It's defined by the construct of this marriage and family.*"

Diego remembered, "In that context, I kept feeding P3, the Picture Perfect Partner, because that's what was expected. That was the milieu in which Ellie felt happiest, and P3 stayed and had a life of his own." And from this construction of the robotic character that was P3 came the construction of the dream of a life that was similarly programmed in its fabrication. With it also came the debut of a new character in Diego's ensemble, *The Dreamer*.

The Dreamer is powerful, inspiring, and compelling, and he, alongside Ellie, constructed a flawlessly curated dream of the perfect marriage, the perfect family. The picture they painted was so convincing that they believed that it was true. There were hints that Diego wasn't as happy as he pretended to be, his vices belying his contentment. And a few perceptive friends had an intuition about the cracks that lay beneath the sheen. But Diego refused to hear anything about it. He was so attached to the picture of how things were supposed to be that he refused to acknowledge how they really were. It would be some time before Diego would shed his rose-colored glasses long enough to recognize the scratches that marred them.

"I started questioning my own behaviors about fifteen years ago as I was doing some personal mastery work, meditation, that kind of thing. I didn't really question my marriage. I assumed that it was me, that it was my problem," Diego recalled. After all, Ellie was the holder of how things should be. She came from the functional family. She had the clear picture of what a successful marriage and family looked like. Diego was the one who needed guidance on how to be a "good" husband and father. Diego surmised that if there was a problem, it must be his.

As Diego continued with his self work and as he came into relationship with Kyra, he began to develop a concept of a self that existed outside of his marriage with Ellie. He recalled, "It's only after I met Kyra and we were in a relationship that I started understanding that my behaviors were not born in isolation, in a desert. They were born in the context of a relationship. Therefore, my marriage was at least in part a cause of what was going on."

Neither Diego nor Ellie could deny the cracks in the dream when Diego's relationship with Kyra blossomed beyond the physical. Diego recalled, "I told Ellie that I was having a relationship with Kyra, and I was in love. I thought this was part of our agreement. It was fine." Clearly Ellie had a different understanding about the nature of the relationships they pursued outside of their marriage. Diego continued, "Ellie pushed back. And I pushed back harder. I said, 'No, I'm not walking away from this.' And I think that was the death of P3. No, not the death. It was the beginning of the agony of P3."

Yet, the Dreamer remained on the stage. He'd just taken up with a different costar. As Diego's and Kyra's relationship deepened, Diego began to dream of a life with Kyra. The Dreamer's powers of inspiration and persuasion were set to work convincing Kyra to embrace the dream, too. Diego recalled, "Over time, the Dreamer created the space for Kyra to consider ending her marriage and making a life with me. The combination of my dreaming about what a life together could be and my ability to create a safe container for her to explore this idea, discuss it with Brock, while not pressing her too hard, giving her as much space as possible, made it possible for her to get to the point where she was willing to consider it."

While the Dreamer took center stage with Kyra, P3, the Picture Perfect Partner, quietly played in the background, subtly reminding Diego of how his actions flew in the face of the person he had constructed himself to be. Ellie, the keeper of what a good marriage and family looks like, still had a hold on Diego. When she gave the ultimatum, "Kyra or me," he tumbled back into his smaller self, grasping at black-and-white options and absolutes and demanding them from Kyra. The spaciousness that he had allowed Kyra as she considered a dream of a life together disappeared in a vacuum. The decision needed to be made now.

The Breaking

Enter the *Cautious Ditherer*.

The Cautious Ditherer was in a constant state of weighing if Diego should stay in his marriage or leave. He came on the scene beckoned by a momentous decision, one with high stakes, particularly in terms of downsides. When push came to shove, when things came to a head, the Cautious Ditherer could not make a choice. Whichever way he looked, the Cautious Ditherer said, "Too much loss here."

The Cautious Ditherer is analytical. He thinks through things from an objective, dispassionate perspective and tries to keep Diego's emotions and feelings at bay. Diego observed, "The way I think about him is that indecision is simply the result of being too fact-based, too objective. It might be that my reluctance to act on a clear-cut analysis of the Cautious Ditherer is a result of my fear that emotion will take over and will lead me down a path that is potentially unacceptable or conventionally reprehensible."

As Diego reflected on the confluence of triggers that threw him into the wormhole of fallback, Diego would name for the first time the script that the Cautious Ditherer had been reading in the background, holding him back from committing to his dream of a relationship with Kyra. Diego wrote to her, "I have come to realize that my worry about the pain and inconvenience of announcing and sorting out the material aspects of divorce has played a big unexamined and unrecognized role in my decision. I am utterly ashamed to admit that questions of expediency have come to distort this vital decision in my life."

When Kyra responded to Diego's request for a decision with swirliness, a decision that Diego himself felt too conflicted to make, *the Wolverine*, teeth bared, bounded on the stage. Diego observed, "The role of the Wolverine was to protect my identity, my dignity, as a way of covering up the fact that I couldn't make a decision. So I think the subterranean logic of it was, *I can't make a decision. I don't want to own up to this. Therefore, my inability to make a decision is her fault because she's not clear enough and she's swirly. Now my Wolverine is going to come and set her straight.*"

Diego was thrown into a smaller, more primal version of himself. Overtaken by self-orientation, he reverted to unilateral forms of power that are primitive and instinctive. Diego felt a loss of control, of power, of certainty and precision. In the win-or-lose scenario Diego had constructed, he saw himself as the loser.

Later, in his letters to Kyra, Diego explained, "I wanted you to indicate to me that you were willing to stretch beyond the scenario you had sketched with Brock. I wanted you to engage with me in the language of power that I need when I am in a corner: boundaries, timelines, alternative scenarios. I felt that I had asked for it multiple times and got no traction. I sorely regretted that you did not attempt to get any closer to my language." When Kyra did not wholesale choose Diego as he longed for her to, Diego responded, "Deal off the table. Not interested."

Diego observed, "The Wolverine did all the fighting and pronounced the 'Fuck you!' But actually, behind the 'Fuck You,' the character who was making the decision to back out was *the Shamed Quitter.*" The Shamed Quitter allows Diego to save face. He blames others, lashes out, and abruptly walks away. Diego explained, "I am not chosen, and that carries with it shame. But in the quitting, there isn't any shame."

Diego would come to realize that the Wolverine and the Shamed Quitter often appeared on stage together. In this scene, when Diego faced into his fear of not winning, of not being in control of a plan that would see him undo his life, his impulse was to score a point to get even, even as he was exiting the relationship.

Over time, as we unearthed the origin stories of Diego's characters, he began to see how frequent their appearances had been over the course of his life, and what caused them to storm the stage when they did. He saw the Cautious Ditherer in his refusal to be pigeon-holed into a particular industry in his career. He located the Wolverine in his early twenties when he was coming of age in a highly competitive environment. He recalled the debut of the Shamed Quitter when his one-time girlfriend later embarked on a romantic relationship with Diego's friend.

He could see these characters still occupying his theater now and could anticipate when they might be beckoned on stage in the future. Having come to know them, he could appreciate the lessons they were there to offer, the parts of himself that they showed up in protection of. He could develop the capacity to cast them intentionally in the scenes of his life, or to put in place the props and scaffolds that made it safe for them not to be there.

Diego proclaimed, "I have by no means liberated myself from the Cautious Ditherer's hold on me. It's a very powerful part of me. It feels even more powerful because I didn't expect it to be there. That's not the image I had of myself. Kyra did not expect it. My friends don't expect it. No one sees me as that. This is sort of a ghost in a closet that showed up. It's sleeping in the shadow, but it wakes up when the boldest decisions are up."

At the time of the fallback, Diego wasn't familiar with the Wolverine. But having named it, he began to realize how familiar it is. He noted, "I absolutely see it. I absolutely sense it rising. But I have it more on a leash. It doesn't just take me over anymore."

As Diego came to know his characters, he discovered the ways in which they do serve him. He could see that the Wolverine played a role in the seductive power that draws people to him. Diego explained, "There is a more primal form of power lurking, and it probably plays a role in the attraction, the charisma, the presence that I project. A tiger lying low but choosing not to pounce."

Diego could see how the Shamed Quitter acted in protection of his dignity. He observed, "In the absence of the Shamed Quitter, I would be sticking with situations in which I am considerably embarrassed and continuously shamed. The Shamed Quitter allows me to get out of situations where the possibility of continued embarrassment exists. It doesn't mean that this character on its own judges the situation right. Clearly, in this case it didn't. But there might be other cases where it does."

Diego paused for a moment, lost in thought, before admitting, "When the Shamed Quitter comes onstage now, there's the blinding insight of, *Fuck! Of course!* There is the embarrassment and disappointment of, *For God's sake! You haven't grown much*. But there's also a smile, right? A smile of recognition, and a smile of acknowledgement, that at least I can see it now as opposed to not being able to see it."

CHAPTER 10
YOUR TURN TO REFLECT

Get to Know Your Cast of Characters

Now is the time to turn inward, to an exploration of and orientation to your inner landscape. Turning our perspective inward allows us to recognize the fluidity and multi-dimensionality of the self and the influence of context (place, time, others also attempting to navigate this world) on who we are able to bring to the table. Through self-reflection during our periods of smallness, we are able to discover the gifts that can only be received from a place of surrender into those earlier but still very present and important aspects of self. We begin to experience how seeking out the gifts of fallback, and accepting them, can allow us to recover, grow, and more deliberately align with our intentions.

Right now, let's commit to recognizing and accepting that we are not consistent in the way we show up. Not on our best days and certainly not now. We are not one, constant, enduring self. We are made up of a multitude of characters comprising a full cast. This, too, is me.

Exercise

Go back and read what you wrote in your freewrite about your experience of grace and your experience of fallback and the gap between the two (from chapter 7), start to finish. As you become familiar with yourself through your writing, circle key words or phrases that stand out to you. Perhaps you are surprised by certain words. Perhaps in reading (and writing) them, they spark emotion—anger when reencountering self in a particular circumstance, sadness about the truth that the word or phrase reveals, contentedness in recognizing a consistent characteristic of who you know yourself to be. Use these words and phrases to identify the characters that have been present in the scenes of your life. Give these characters names that are meaningful to you.

Now select one of the characters you identified—perhaps the one that, if you could get a handle on it, would make the biggest difference in how you show up in your life and relationships. Think of two to three examples of scenes from your present or past that this character has been prominent in. Take a few minutes to write a description of the scene.

What was the context in which this character showed up? What were the circumstances? What cued this character to come on stage? What was it like to play this character? Where is this character most welcome? By whom? In which scenes is this character least welcome? What makes it so?

Looking across all of the scenes, what is similar about these? What is different? Has your experience of the character changed over time? What new discoveries have you made as you locate this character in these scenes?

Set a timer for ten minutes and write about this.

Remember, it can be tempting to seek to deny the small self. To think about the characters that came on the scene when we were not at our best and say, "That's not me. That's just the circumstance." Often when we experience fallback, we tend to think of it as this isolated occurrence, an isolated encounter with this stranger. We say to ourselves, "Whoa, who is this rogue character? Where did you come from?" But if we're honest with ourselves, we likely know these characters well, even if they are not the characters that we generally want to be known as. Yet, this, too, is us. We are both heroes and villains. And in claiming the fullness of us, we allow these smaller parts of self to loosen their grip. We come into relationship and truth and authenticity with ourselves and with others.

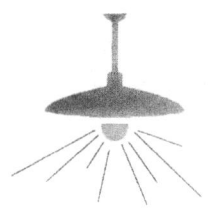

CHAPTER 11
RECOGNIZING TRIGGERS

As humans, we are incredibly complex and unique. The thing that tethers me back to my smaller self—that part of me that does not contain my full capacities to think, feel, or behave in a way that meets my intentions—may be different than what prompts fallback in you. Yet understanding some of the overarching triggers for fallback may help us better anticipate when our ability to bring our bigger self to a scene may be threatened and also help us to understand what it is our fallback characters are trying to protect us from.

An understanding of the interaction between psychology (the study of the human mind and behavior) and neuroscience (the study of the anatomy and physiology of the brain) may offer us greater appreciation for the whole system that is at play when we are triggered into fallback and the whole thing seems to go down.

Brain scientist David Rock identified five domains of human experience that motivate threat and reward responses in the brain. The domains that make up his SCARF model include: S = status—how one is perceived by others; C = certainty—ability to predict the future; A = autonomy/freedom—sense of control and of having choices; R = relatedness—sense of safety with others; F = fairness—sense that exchanges between people are fair.[1] In essence, threats to status, certainty, autonomy and freedom, relatedness, and fairness, as well as those related to safety and survival—having our basic needs met—can lead to the experience of being taken over by a less complex way of making meaning, of feeling destabilized and at psychological risk.

When we feel threatened, our amygdala, the part of our brain where emotion and primitive flight-fight responses are housed, goes on high alert. The amygdala, when triggered by threat, can override the neocortex where cognition, our conscious processing, resides. Under threat, the brain adopts less-refined responses, retreating to what's safe, eschewing the perspectives and broader options that it, in the moment of threat, perceives as dangerous.[2]

Effectively, there is a biochemical response to certain stimuli that may temporarily not allow us to access the cognitive developmental tools that may constitute our better self. The protective mechanism of our brain, honed over thousands of years, causes our cognitive mind to go on lockdown.

At times when we fall back, our sense of certainty, safety, and security feels threatened, as so often happened with Robbin over the course of the pandemic. Sometimes the threat is to our freedom and sense of fairness, as was the case with Octavia. And other times when we find ourselves in fallback, our status and relatedness feel at risk, as they did with Diego. Threats to the five SCARF areas reduce our capacity to collaborate and persuade, limit empathy and feelings of connectedness, and cause us to become emotional, to act more impulsively, and to resist change.[3] In short, our brain hijacks our mind.

Perhaps this is the physiological explanation for why certain circumstances, particularly those tied to one's primitive self (e.g., those involving family) or involving risk (e.g., illness, injury, threat, fear) nearly inevitably catalyze fallback. Understanding that there is a biological brain response that is often activated when we are in fallback, and that the ghosts that rush the stage are protecting a self that feels at risk, may offer us more compassion for ourselves and others when we fall back.

In my research on fallback, I identified four overarching triggers for fallback: contextual gravitational pulls, challenges to identity, unresolved trauma, and the triggers inherent in the ordinary navigation of life.[4]

Contextual Gravitational Pulls

When our rational mind is not being trumped by the primal part of our brain, we each possess a set of capacities and a seat from which we make sense of the world and our place in it most of the time. When we make meaning from this *center of gravity*, our actions, thoughts, and feelings are aligned with our intentions. We often think of this as our better self.

Just as individuals have certain developmental capacities, so do families, communities, teams, organizations, and cultures. Each of these systems has its own center of gravity. Occasionally, the contextual center of gravity is a little out ahead of your own, prompting you to learn and grow, see more complexity, become bigger. This is often referred to as the leading edge. It's the new pair of soccer cleats that your child can't wait to grow into. At other times, the surrounding center of gravity of your environment matches your developmental level. It supports you being exactly where you are in your ability to take perspective and address complexity. It's warm and cozy and feels like your favorite old robe. But in some cases, the center of gravity of our systems, relationships, teams, organizations, states, nation, or culture is smaller than we are. It feels pinching and restrictive. It's the prom dress you try to fit into twenty years later.

These systems and their developmental capacities exert a powerful gravitational pull on our individual capacities. As those in our families are experiencing fallback, the center of gravity of the family system dips. As we talk to our neighbors or our colleagues, or sift through our social media feeds, or read the news, we feel our own sense of self, the world, and our place in it shrinking.[5]

Contexts, relationships, systems, and narratives have a way of reinforcing the self that they have known us to be. They are invested in that self. Change and deviation are scary to those who surround us, particularly if one person is changing while the other(s) remain in stasis. They wonder, *Where are you going? And why? Aren't we doing fine right here?* Accordingly, we are powerfully influenced by the gravitational pull of the contexts surrounding us, and they exert an even stronger pull as we attempt to escape their force.

We see this playing out in Diego's relationship with his wife Ellie and the influence of the gravitational pull of their marital system on his capacities in "the breaking" with Kyra. Diego was not only pulled between two women but pulled between two developmental contexts. There was the gravitational pull of Ellie, who had throughout their relationship served as the exemplar of *the way things should be* in family and marriage, a vision that was black-and-white and marked by certainty, and one that Diego had for many years doggedly sought and adhered to. And then there was the developmental gravitational pull of Kyra in all of her swirliness, who saw and offered possibilities for intimacy in many forms, many as yet undefined.

Though Diego could see beyond a black-and-white, absolute orientation in other areas of his life, within the confines of his marriage, the tether was still powerful. As Diego grew in his complexity and sense-making and through his relationship with Kyra, he had begun to probe the contours of his marriage to Ellie and his wholesale devotion to it as good, adequate, right. Yet Ellie, the keeper of what a good marriage looks like, still had a hold on him. When Ellie gave the ultimatum, "Kyra or me," Diego tumbled back into an earlier self, grasping at conventions and demanding them from Kyra.

Diego's Picture Perfect Partner (P3) and the Cautious Ditherer danced in the stage wings during his fallback with Kyra. Diego's P3, formed through years in a context that made explicit the social and familial conditions for acceptance, tethered him to an earlier way of making sense and acting in the context of his marriage. And the Cautious Ditherer was hesitant to commit to an untested and undefined plan for a future with Kyra that would have him undo his life. The contextual gravitational pull from both sides created a tear that sent him tumbling into the wormhole of fallback.

Contextual gravitational pulls sweep the ground out from under us and propel us into the basement of our sense-making. But our contexts are not the only factor contributing to the variability of our capacities. Development itself is an intricate structure. And if not solidly and consistently supported, it can be blown over by the wind, leaving us on the ground of our earliest structures, searching the debris for the parts of us that existed before.

Challenges to Identity

Challenges to identity cause us to not recognize the person we have known ourselves to be. They may take the form of major life events, new experiences, or disorienting dilemmas.

Major life events that catalyze fallback may include unemployment, bad marriages, the death of a loved one, illness or injury. However, it's not only seemingly negative events that challenge our sense of who we know ourselves to be. Berger referred to new experiences such as new parenthood, taking a new job, and moving to a new country as "rich learning zones." She noted the paradox that these seemingly positive circumstances, those that are often cited by the theorists as catalyzing developmental growth, allow us to be in touch with our full capacities, both big and small. Major life events, whether perceived as positive or negative, significantly challenge one's identity and trigger feelings of loss of control.[6]

Disorienting dilemmas are experiences that transform or challenge our perspectives, unsettle our meaning-making, add complexity, and cause cognitive dissonance. In these situations, our normal biases are no longer adequate for describing reality.[7] Disorienting dilemmas peppered all facets of our lives during the Covid-19 pandemic and its corresponding lockdown.

There were things in the past, values-based things, that we could ignore, that we had ignored. In the hecticness that had marked the normal course of life, we would get distracted from the niggling feeling that things weren't right. We didn't have enough attention to give to them, enough time. There was something about the pandemic experience that points of incongruence became no longer just nagging annoyances, or a pesky discomfort in the stomach, but a full-on gut punch.

During pandemic times, the confluence of disorienting dilemmas, major life events, and new experiences set the stage for massive and recurring challenges to identity. The circumstances were so intense, the contrast between our preferred image of self and how we were actually showing up was so stark, that the façade was bound to collapse. Robbin, like so many others of us, was repeatedly brought face-to-face with the ways he was not who he imagined or painted himself to be. Though he tried mightily to deny it, he eventually was forced to witness and accept the toppling in plain sight of the self he had constructed.

When Robbin suddenly found himself a full-time caretaker to his two small children, with his powers of accompaniment directed only to the three other people who made up his household, he was unable to locate himself. The person who he had known himself to be, the person he longed to be *out there*, had disappeared in the trap door of the stage of his pandemic life. Yet Robbin still expected to be the same person, with the same capacities, and to see himself in the same way. But the set had changed, as did the people who were cast as his most frequent costars. When the reality of Robbin's life didn't match up with the storyline that he had written, Robbin's sense of self went into freefall.

How we are able to be seen is dependent upon who we are in relationship with. I may be funny or smart or a deep and curious listener in one relationship and those parts of my identity may not be expressed, or at least may not be capable of being seen and received, in relationship with another. Relationships are the context in which our identity is formed. If you remove the individual from these identity-forming relationships, the center of gravity of identity is thrown out of whack. You can see that you were this, but in it's not being recognized by others, you begin to wonder if it is lost. When we lose who we have known ourselves to be, who we have been seen as, we wonder if we, too, will cease to exist.

Unresolved Trauma

The present exerts a powerful force on our physiological, cognitive, emotional, and psychological self. Yet, our past also mightily influences how we are able to meet this moment and see ourselves in it. Unresolved trauma refers to trauma that we may have experienced at an earlier time in life, an earlier time in our development, when we may have been constructing the world in a simpler way.

At the time it occurred, we may not have had the capacity to resolve it with the developmental capacities with which we were then equipped. In order to survive the situation, perhaps we found a way to remove ourselves from it. That has a big cost in that some part of our experience may have gotten bracketed off. The rest of self develops and becomes more complex, while the bracketed self is left at that earlier historical and developmental time.

That way of meaning is preserved until we are psychologically strong enough and have the developmental capability to reintegrate the parts of self that were left behind. Until then, whenever we encounter someone or something that resembles that trauma, we fall back to that earlier stage of development, of meaning-making, of that truth when it first occurred.[8]

When we re-encounter our unresolved trauma, we find ourselves in a hyper-alert state, constantly on the lookout for threats. There can be a literal or psychological feeling of our life being at risk.

As Octavia reflected on her fallback, she came to realize that while her competence felt threatened in the interactions with Brenda, it was her freedom that felt most at risk. "Freedom is a very important thing for me," Octavia noted. "I mean it actually is *really important*. It is for a lot of people, but for me it is *really, really important*. It is important for me to have a sense of choice and autonomy and flexibility and creativity."

Octavia explained, "I'm one of the few people I know who hated being a child, because I felt like I did not have control over my environment or the situations I was in. So even if I'm going through difficulty, I can deal with that as long as I have chosen difficulty, and as long as I feel like I have freedom and choice and I can move out of things if I need to."

In the meetings with Brenda during which she critiqued Octavia's projects without a willingness to hear a different perspective, without even acknowledging Octavia's presence and addressing her directly, Octavia felt as if her personhood was not respected. Octavia recalled, "I have been in work environments in my early years where I felt trapped, and where I felt controlled, working for bosses or people who were not humane, where I didn't have a voice." Octavia felt the work environment did not allow for her full self and was smothering.

Octavia noted, "If I feel like I can't influence the situation, it becomes very challenging for me. I want to go. There's a part of me that always needs to have an escape hatch. The one who wants to flee is really about how I have agency and freedom in spaces where I feel powerless. There is an underlying thread that has something to do with feeling trapped, being mistreated or taken advantage of somehow, and being able to protect myself and get out of situations. That actually has been a huge theme for me across jobs, across relationships." Octavia began looking for the nearest fire exit.

In my experience, fallback triggered by unresolved trauma has a particular flavor, thrust, and stickiness to it. My sense is that fallback triggered by a person or thing that is reminiscent of the experience of the original trauma subsumes the entire self. There's force in this kind of fallback, a throwing back, if you will.

The tether created by unresolved trauma has a particular grip because we didn't trudge through all of the developmental terrain necessary to grow that part of self. In protection of us, an *us* that was incapable at the time of facing into trauma, that part of self remained encapsulated or bracketed off as the rest of us developed. Until such time that we are able, from our more complex self, to re-encounter, embrace, and guide that aspect of self, we will continue to be at its mercy.[9]

Ordinary Triggers

Ordinary triggers of fallback prompt a passive digression into more habitual, less strategic, less complex developmental capacities. Ordinary triggers may take the form of the mundane, everyday conditions of life, including overwork, group norms, stress, exhaustion, tension, and hunger. They also encompass more intense experiences, such as depression, rage, failure, illness, fear, shame, and loss. Circumstances of uncertainty, ambiguity, and complexity also fall under the category of ordinary triggers of fallback. When activated by ordinary triggers, we often feel our capacities slipping away.[10]

In my experience of fallback with my children at the restaurant, the ordinary factors of life sent me spiraling into a smaller self. I was exhausted from not having slept well for months. The stress of the herculean task I had been given at work and the seemingly impossible timeframe for accomplishing it overwhelmed me. My sense of responsibility—imposed on me by others, yes, but also which I had largely loaded on myself—were smothering, eliminating the joy from most everything I engaged in, including my interactions with my children. I was ashamed not to be able to hold it all and to do so without breaking a sweat. Instead, most days I was crumbling in a puddle on the floor. And in that very moment as we sat in the crowded restaurant with achingly slow service, I was hungry. The ordinary triggers of life conspired to take me down!

The experience of fallback that I recounted could easily be dismissed as one sparked by the ordinary triggers, the natural confluence of life. It could be seen as only a transitory dip, something that happened in a moment before life went on. Yet, as I recall this episode now seven years later, my stomach tightens, my heart feels heavy, and tears spill from my eyes. I am sad about that moment of fallback and the hundreds of other moments like it that have taken place with my children over the years precipitated by the normal triggers of life, often in concert—as was the case in this situation—with the other triggers that were at play (e.g. contextual gravitational pulls, challenges to identity). Establishing a relationship with my fallback, no matter what the presenting catalyst for it, welcoming it onto the stage, and inviting it to teach me, compels me to inquire more deeply.

After all, when we explore people's occasions of fallback, a transitory dip into one's full range is very often the experience. It may feel like a passing, surface reaction to passing, surface circumstances. Yet, when we explore what underlies these reactions, we often find that the fallback is connected to something much deeper and more enduring.

Herein lies the value in cultivating a relationship with our fallback. Herein lies the value in counting as fallback these ordinary triggers and the commonplace occurrence of our living into our full range, including the earlier parts. When we pay attention to even our passing experiences of showing up a smaller version of self rather than set it aside as something that just is, we open up our capacity to work with it, to begin to notice it, to explore what it's about for us.

Our triggers for fallback exert a powerful pull on the self, beckoning characters on stage that we did not cast in the play. The contexts we live and work in are not always in alignment with our own bigger capacities, thereby pulling us back in their gravitational force. We encounter illness, death and birth, new bosses and job changes, moves to foreign lands, and, yes, even pandemics that lock out or alter or deconstruct the parts of self and identity that formed us. We come face-to-face with a way of knowing the world that unsettles our meaning-making and challenges who we have known ourselves to be and who we wish to be seen as. The younger parts in us that detached from our developmental path so that the rest of us might continue to grow continue to linger in the wings, thrust onto the stage when we encounter a thing or person who resembles a trauma from earlier in our lives, or in the lives of those who came before us.

And then there are just the conditions of life as a human living in these times. Our full physiological and psychological capacities are not always going to be present to us. The circumstances of our surround that bolster our bigger selves will not always be erected. The ordinary triggers of life will trip us up and cause us to fall back.

It is important to understand these triggers so that we may recognize them in ourselves as we walk through the field of our current existence. The value of understanding fallback is in its capacity to remind us that we need to be diligent to our own development, to minding the way we show up in the world and measuring it against the way we believe we show up. We must do this without shame or judgment but with a commitment to reflection. A critical component of recognizing fallback is recognizing the triggers that prompt it in us.

CHAPTER 12
ROBBIN RECOGNIZING TRIGGERS

Throughout this chapter, we will come to know some of the characters that comprised Robbin's cast during the first year of the pandemic. We will witness his discovery of the scenes of his life, past and present, where these characters originated and were further developed. And we will identify the triggers that beckoned these characters onto the stage of his life, be they the ordinary circumstances that made up life in lockdown, the gravitational pull of a context formed by quarantine with two small children and an overworked spouse, the challenges to identity posed by circumstances in which Robbin was unable to locate the person he had known himself to be, or the unresolved trauma that was ever present in a world that turned on its head the safeguards that protected Robbin from the foreboding and forbidden aspects of self, long stitched over and locked away.

In his first take on identifying characters, Robbin named the Joy Protector, the Opportunity Runner, the Genius Connector, the Turf Roarer, and the Shame Trapper. We have seen glimpses of some of these characters in the descriptions of Robbin's acute fallback experiences in the context of pandemic, quarantine, and home life with his small children, and the dissolution of professional life as a result of all of these. Over the course of the next nine months, through our explorations, additional characters would emerge from the shadows to be illuminated by the ghost light, some who had been banished from the theater during its early days, others who were just a niggling notion of a character that was coming into being.

The Joy Protector

The Joy Protector tried mightily to commandeer the stage to make the experience of the pandemic joyful, to make Robbin's family's experience of a dark time something that beautiful memories could be made of. Often, Robbin's protection of joy manifested in cooking elaborate meals. The kitchen became his respite, the place where he could locate a part of himself that he could recognize while also feeding the souls and the bellies of his family.

Robbin noted, "I remember the first few weeks thinking *how can we turn this into something that the kids will love?* That was front and center for me. I was spending a lot of mental energy on being there for my kids to have them grow through the experience."

For a while, it seemed to be working. Robbin continued, "As devastating as everything was, if you ask my son, who's a better correspondent than my daughter for their experience right now, he thinks coronavirus time, despite having limited interaction with the world around him, is fun. He's gotten a ton of attention. And I can see that that is a function of the time that I spent with him. Even though my experience of coronavirus time is vastly different, I don't take issue with his experience of it. I see where he's coming from, and I totally get it. So it's like don't burst that bubble."

"But at the same time, I think the part that messes with my identity is that I think what I should be doing and what I should be giving extends far beyond my four walls. And I feel like there's something missing for only having it go here."

Before long, Robbin's longing to be and do more beyond the confines of his family overwhelmed his capacity to make coronavirus time joyful for his kids. The ordinary triggers that were ever present during pandemic times—exhaustion, stress, uncertainty, depression, and fear—combined with Robbin's inability to do the things that had comprised his identity and defined his existence, were shackles on Robbin's capacities.

"I think the Joy Protector is very much part of me and who I am, but I don't think he was ever called on to perform for quite as much of a sustained engagement." Robbin noted, "We might see little blips when Linda needs to sleep in on the weekend, and it's time to make waffles and keep everyone entertained and out of her hair. But doing that for weeks on end was a new experience that turned me inside out."

Robbin observed, "I've relied on the Joy Protector in the past, taking for granted that he gets sourced, that he gets energized in ways that hasn't happened this time round. Apparently, the fuel available to him is not an endless supply and runs out pretty quickly when not taken care of." Without the aspects of life that protected joy for and within him, without the ability to have a light shown on these other aspects of self, another character began to take over.

Robbin recalled, "One evening, I was exhausted. My wife was trying to feel human, so I was making sure that the kids didn't bother her first thing in the morning. I was getting three meals on the table throughout the weekend. And I was worn down. And after cooking a dinner that I was super proud of, that was supposed to mimic a diner—burgers and home-cut fries, banana peanut butter shakes—I decided we would call my mom. She had sent these beautiful clothes for the kids. And I thought, why don't we bestow these outfits to them through a ceremony and talk about what they had done well just to make it extra special and peg these outfits to memories of good behavior."

But Robbin had overlooked the need to account for the ordinary triggers that had become permanent props on the set of his life during pandemic. Daily life had become marked by uncertainty and risk, rage and shame. When he tried to orchestrate a video chat with the kids and his mom following a long weekend of tending to others, ordinary triggers peppered the stage. Robbin was exhausted. He was having a hard time putting two thoughts together. Yet, he had high expectations for how this interaction would go. He had scripted the whole thing in his head but hadn't thought to share the lines with the other actors.

"It's the children who have their own little boisterous agenda, the parent who doesn't hear everything and often requires me to translate, add to that bad connectivity, and the fact that I'm exhausted. And I'm very much attached to a good outcome from this interaction."

Robbin recalled, "We call my mom, and then Charles interrupts her. And I have such a short fuse that any interruption is going to cause me to bark, 'Charles, don't do that!' And then Linda, who has zero tolerance for anyone barking, walks out. And I just spiraled down. I was so ashamed. I like to shine. I like to be seen as a beacon in my family. And I knew in that moment that I had blown it. I was inconsolable for the rest of the evening."

Robbin admitted, "I just thought, it's worked every day up till now. And so much was working every day up till now that I kind of took for granted that of course things would work. In truth, I think the expectation that I can just walk onto the stage and have things go the way I want them, probably anytime, but especially now, is like sauntering up to a gas station and lighting up a cigarette. It's begging for trouble."

Robbin continued, "When Charles does something that to me seems really dangerous, he often says, 'But nothing happened.' And I say, 'You know why nothing happened? You were lucky!' And I think that's something that I need to be telling myself when I am able to serve dinner and pull off an intricate call at the same time. 'You know why shit didn't blow up in your face? Because you were lucky. Not because of any special skill on your part. "You just got lucky this time."'"

During the pandemic and the associated lockdown, we were forced to recognize that those things that we could just go in and do unthinking, that worked out because we were lucky or because the circumstances in our surround somehow supported, at this time, in our environment, those circumstances didn't exist anymore.

Even when we are not in a constant state of fear, uncertainty, exhaustion, and loss—which we frequently were during the pandemic—these ordinary triggers are present and sneak onto the stage of our daily lives. Even in the best of times, we can't expect that our bigger self will show up without the scaffolds in place to support it.

Robbin observed, "One filter that I've been viewing most things through is all or nothing. What does that mean in terms of the fallback? Well, it could mean that if I have this expectation that all of my days are 10 out of 10, it might be best to realize that all I'm ever going to hit right now is an 8. And so how do you behave on a day that can't be better than an 8, where being an 8 requires a lot of making expectations explicit? Ratchet down expectations, but also do a lot of work in order to actually meet the ratcheted down expectations."

Perhaps we need to ask ourselves, what is it going to take for me to show up aligned with my intentions? What from the bottom tiers of Maslow's hierarchy of needs must be present for me to do the thing that I think I should just be able to walk on stage and do? And sometimes they are not going to be present, so maybe the show's not going to go on tonight. Because I just can't bring it.

The Turf Roarer

During the pandemic, Robbin was quite literally locked out of the physical places where his normal daily functioning took place while simultaneously being locked out of the psychological contexts that propped up his bigger self. The kinds of structures and supports that lend themselves to Robbin's best behaviors, his highest capacities, were taken away. The context that Robbin lived in alongside his two small children and wife was in lockdown, and he was pulled back in its gravitational force.

Robbin likened the shrinking of his physical and psychological space to being pulled into a vortex. He wistfully recalled life before the pandemic. "It was just a given that I could slide into my day and find those protected spaces. But now I have to create them on purpose, knowing that I create them on purpose. It was unthinking before."

And moment by moment, the expectations of how his life would be, how he would be in it, were dashed. Day by day, there was a shrinking of experience, of possibilities. Existence was marked by uncertainty. Life was suddenly unscripted.

As Robbin's sense of agency and choice were taken away, as he was removed from the adult interactions and spaciousness that fed his soul, Robbin's context and his interior sense-making shrunk. In this pandemic, there was no space or time or welcoming context to be the Robbin that he had known himself to be and that he had coveted being seen as. The Turf Roarer barged onto the stage in protection of whatever ground he had left to stand on, and it was fast disappearing.

The Turf Roarer disrupted the scene when Charles interrupted his grandmother post burgers-and-shakes dinner. He reared his head in fury when Elsa punched Robbin in the nose. He raged at the landlord when she came to collect the ten months of remaining rent on an office that Robbin would never again step foot in. The Turf Roarer roared at most every invasion of Robbin's turf as Robbin attempted to wrest control and safety from a context seemingly devoid of both.

Robbin admitted, "The Turf Roarer left to his own devices will turn my kids into enemies. It seems the most distant and primitive of them all. The one who doesn't have the right to show up in a polished space. And what's most remarkable is the amount of energy I invest in not being aware of this. Being on the defensive doesn't square with my self-image, so I don't *think* I do this. I do it a lot."

Aside from the undeniable-in-their-scope-and-impact displays of rage, Robbin, in the beginning, had a hard time seeing the Turf Roarer as more than a character who popped in for a rare guest appearance. In time, Robbin came into acceptance of the Turf Roarer as a significant player in his full ensemble. He observed, "Our exploration helped me see something really remarkable—I do a lot more roaring than I think. When a kid crawls onto my body, I ask them to get off, and when they don't, my voice gets louder. It's not being able to have the physical outcome that I want that triggers the desperation, that triggers the yelling, because it feels like I'm running out of options. My sense of turf gets cramped a lot."

Much as the Turf Roarer was not an expression of self that Robbin was proud of, he could see the character's value given the context Robbin was living in. Robbin noted, "The Turf Roarer shows up as me getting excited and yelling so I don't have to face existential questions. It's like, keep things simple here. Don't make me question whether I'm providing. Don't make me question whether I'm caring. The Turf Roarer showing up in this capacity at this time has maintained a certain level of equilibrium. Could I improve on the arrangement that my life is? Yes. Does the Turf Roarer prevent that? Yes. You know, it's a keeping-things-going, and we all have a keep-things-going mode. That's what I think it is."

Yet, the yelling that characterized the Turf Roarer, while a frequent feature of life during lockdown, had not always been Robbin's orientation. In fact, before the pandemic, Robbin was averse to anger. He recalled, "I remember in couples therapy before Linda and I got married, one of the things that surfaced was just how touchy anger was to me. I would rather go dopey or just kind of turn off. If anger swelled up, it was like a kill switch that turned me off. But there's just so much anger right now that that's not even an option. Because I need to function even as I experience anger. There's no just going catatonic for two days." The contextual gravitational pull of pandemic life swept the Turf Roarer onto the stage in protection of survival, of functioning, of just getting Robbin's family through another day.

As things spiraled out of Robbin's control, when he became desperate, expressing anger felt like the only option for having it recognized. As the pandemic closed in on his sense of self and the world he lived in, as he felt powerless to do anything about it, Robbin began to own his rage. And because of the circumstances and demands of life during a pandemic, there was no spaciousness in either his external or internal reality. The intrusions on his turf were constant and unyielding, and he roared in anguish and defense of the ground he was losing, that the world seemed to be losing.

The Drowning

"I tapped into something more primal even than a Turf Roarer," read the text I received from Robbin. "I'll just call him the Drowning. That's what the Turf Roarer protects. I yell to avoid obliteration. But obliteration is its own character. And he was present. This is some tender-ass stuff."

Robbin experienced the Drowning as a loss of capacity, a shrinking, a shift from consuming life wholly to not being able to wake up. Robbin felt destitute, overwhelmed, with no energy to bring to anyone or anything else. It was survival, but on life support. The Drowning represented a succumbing to the chipping away of the identity that Robbin had spent a lifetime erecting.

At the beginning of the pandemic, Robbin had big ideas for how he could contribute to helping others make sense of the topsy-turvy world that was 2020. He had spent his career preparing himself to be of service to people in ways that would allow them to meet this moment. But as the groundhog days of pandemic life played on repeat, he didn't have the capacity, the time, the energy, or the focus to be able to see any of these ideas through. All the while, he was watching those around him thrive doing just that and felt left behind. As he was pursuing and would eventually earn the credential that would verify his unique capacity to contribute to the world in this way, he simultaneously found his hands tied to do so. After all of the preparation, he was not cast in the role he had trained for.

Robbin felt that if he wasn't contributing to the betterment of the world, he must be contributing to its ruin. Perhaps this was an even starker reckoning in 2020, when the world seemed to be in shambles.

In our explorations, he often invoked a variation on Descartes's "I think, therefore I am." In the before times, Robbin constructed himself as "I X, therefore I am." Now, in the absence of X, he was no longer. Robbin discovered that his was a conditional existence. The Drowning was triggered by Robbin's inability to locate the self he had been.

Robbin noted, "Being a middle-aged dude who's ostensibly at the pinnacle of his profession and pointing that at kindergarten is not a good fit. It's just a horrible mismatch that does damage to the tool that is me." Robbin did a fair job of showing up well on the outside most of the time, but he was being torn apart on the inside as a result of not being able to bring his gifts to bear in the places where he most wanted, as a result of not being able to see himself as the person he had known himself to be.

He continued, "It has been devastating just to see how these responsibilities rule out anything but a vestigial, part-time professional role. I feel like there's something huge that I could and should be contributing right now, and it's not in the cards. I can get intellectually how maybe providing for my family this year is making sure that our son gets through it with a love of learning. And yet there are the parts of me that define my existence differently. And there's a jet lag there. How do I catch up to that?"

"The words that come to me are shock and awe," remarked Robbin. "If that's not happening, then there's that part of me that wonders if it's even there. And I think work provided an outlet to that for many years. I could have a conversation and impress someone. And I think it's not just shocking another, but also myself. If I'm not getting that high, I'm wondering if I exist. It's like needing to stick your fingers in the socket, just to make sure you can still feel."

Robbin reflected, "The whole pandemic experience is kind of like a curtain on what I was doing before. I've gone through life, particularly the last decade, super focused on other people, super focused on always being in touch with and communicating with. And I entered this pandemic wanting to be there for and be there with others. But as I had fewer and fewer of Maslow's building blocks, I was recognizing just how limited my energy was. And it made me realize that if not dependence on others, at least propensity to turn to others may have been a holdover from a time when I didn't need to concentrate my energy in so focused a manner on people within my own four walls. And the demands in here were so great that it overrode everything else."

The Drowning forced Robbin to focus on the bottom tier of Maslow's pyramid—safety, survival, sustenance. He circled the wagons in protection of himself and his family, and in so doing, he shut out those things that made him bigger. Robbin admitted, "I know there are things that might be helpful in getting me out. And I just can't bring myself to even try them on. I just didn't have the energy to reach out to someone. Having a conversation, taking the time to do anything, was a zero-sum game."

When the Drowning came on stage, Robbin had no strength to bring to anyone or anything else. "I think in its less-extreme forms, it kicks me into a mode of automaticity. Just get shit done. But when it's more extreme, my contributions start falling off. I really can't help with putting anyone to bed. I can't get things done. My efforts dry up. My ability to effort dries up. It feels like *I can't*. The Drowning character is kind of like Cameron at the beginning of *Ferris Bueller's Day Off*. Just helpless. Like it's all for naught. No access to agency. The Drowning protects life. It closes down efforting when efforting may be counterproductive."

The Drowning had been there all along, waiting in the wings as the Joy Protector's energy waned, as Robbin slowly withdrew from his professional interactions, as aspects of Robbin's identity dried up, as preservation, pure and simple, became the end game. But Robbin had not yet invited him into the light. Even now, he only acknowledged the Drowning when he collapsed in a heap on the stage of his life.

Though Robbin had not named the character until now, he would soon realize that the pandemic was not the Drowning's debut performance. He recalled a period just a couple of years prior, after Elsa was born, when a confluence of events conspired to beckon the Drowning onto the stage of his life. Robbin remembered, "It started with all of the grandparents being in the same place when Elsa was born. And particularly on my side, them needing attention and help rather than being able to offer it. And having my divorced mom and dad in the same place and having to navigate that is bullshit."

"And on top of that, Charles came down with hand, foot, and mouth disease when Elsa was two weeks old. And so it became my job to keep my three-and-a-half-year-old son, who wanted nothing but to be around his new baby sister, away from her. Of course, I had to quarantine from her, too. And then I got it, obviously, because when someone is slobbering on you in the middle of the night, there's not much you can do about not getting saliva on yourself."

"So that was a brutal kickoff to that summer during which my business suffered. And in the middle of that summer, Linda had a very pointed talk with me about how if I can't pull it together on the business end of things, our unit is threatened. I can't even remember the particulars of it or exactly what was said. But the contours are, *Your inability to provide financially threatens our family*. That's the in-my-bones takeaway. And that is like an arrow straight into my own sense of obliteration right there. And while she's disavowed anything about that statement since then, and attributed it to postpartum—'that was not me'—I can't unsee it."

There was a convergence of factors that beckoned the Drowning on stage both then and now. The ordinary triggers of illness, exhaustion, stress, and overwhelm. The contextual gravitational pulls to a smaller physical and psychological space in the isolation with the family Robbin had created (now) and his family of origin (then), both pulling him into a trappedness in their own unique ways. There were the challenges to identity of not being able to see or be seen as the person Robbin had known himself to be.

And there was unresolved trauma inherited throughout the course of Robbin's childhood.

Robbin's father was a dreamer. He had lofty ideas but was throughout his life unable to channel them into a method for providing for his family. Robbin recalled, "My dad just figured out every possible angle to keep his head in the clouds without ever actually providing financially or emotionally for the people around him. This led to a horrible marriage to my mom, strife, and a very long and protracted divorce."

When Robbin was ten, in the heat of his parents' divorce, his maternal grandfather took him aside and told him that the kind of man that Robbin needed to be was one that was unlike his father. Robbin's grandfather made clear to him that love and acceptance in his family looked like contributing and providing, something that Robbin's father had never done. Robbin carried this "truth" with him and claimed it as his own from that point forward.

Robbin remembered, "That event and others resulted in me having a very tangled relationship to love within my family. Love means not being like my father. And love also means trying to have a relationship with him, not in view of everybody else. I think that finding my own path and developing my own career and persona has been a tension between navigating those guidelines and completely rejecting them. It's an ever-present polarity."

These other-imposed expectations calcified into a self-imposed identity that was entangled with the right to be loved, to be trusted, a right that Robbin would relinquish to others for their bestowal throughout his life. Robbin proclaimed, "Maybe the struggle to even accept myself is the real kicker. Maybe I have self-acceptance pegged to the authority that my grandfather exerted on me at the time; to the authority I let Linda exert on me. That particular part of my life is not in my own authoritative grasp. Maybe there's something about my right to be loved, I just want to hold it in trust to them. And it's a dicey proposition."

When Robbin's financial contributions were coming up short the summer that Elsa was born, and he couldn't see a way to right the boat, Robbin felt obliteration coming on. The Drowning was rapping at the stage door. Robbin observed, "I think it's a bottoming out of faith. If we organize our lives to avoid certain things, I think a lot of my life is organized around avoiding my parents' divorce and seeing any echoes or ripples of it."

When the pandemic struck and Robbin's sense of self shrunk to tending only to the daily functioning of the four people living in his house, the *you better start contributing* script, both his own and those from his past, played in his head. Robbin explained, "We can have rational conversations about how, yes, right now, it is my role to step back professionally and be there for our kids, for Charles in particular and his education. And I still can't unsee that conversation. So it's walking that line. I can't reconcile what I need to do and how I'm actually going to accomplish that. And I'm not. And I'm not. And I'm not. And I think that it's the *and I'm not* that has some kind of connection with the sense of drowning."

The pulls on who Robbin *should* be were felt from every angle, his ancestors and his offspring. One aspect of Robbin's identity lived in the story that his grandfather had written for him and that Linda reinforced following Elsa's birth. Love was not being like his father. In order to be and give love, Robbin needed to have a purpose, provide financially for his family, deliver something meaningful to the world. When these things were swept away in the pandemic squall, at least these things in the form that his grandfather envisioned them and that Robbin had come to prize himself, Robbin was thrust into fallback. Robbin's inability to provide in the ways that he thought he should, that he was told he must, felt like a betrayal of love. And this translated into petulant behavior, overcompensation by cooking, and realizing that this doesn't equal the kind of providing that deserves love.

Providing for his family looked different now than it did in the past. Yet he continued to work from the old storyline written by his grandfather, subsumed by the unresolved trauma that bracketed off that part of self in Robbin's youth. Not providing in the ways he was told he must felt like a threat to his family system with Robbin at fault.

In Robbin's construction of a world in which *I X, therefore I am*, in the absence of X, there was no *I am*. Robbin felt he had lost himself, that he no longer existed. He sunk into the obliteration brought on stage by the Drowning.

The Shame Trapper

As Robbin's fears rose of not being seen and respected by the people he loves, of not being worthy of love, the Shame Trapper exploded onto the stage. Robbin felt as if unfair demands were being made of him during pandemic times. He had to give up so much of himself, who he knew himself to be, the parts that he loved, in order to tend to his family. And this version of tending to his family looked nothing like that which his grandfather had told him made him worthy of love.

"The Shame Trapper comes out when things aren't going the way I'd like them to go," observed Robbin. "I feel powerless, angry, and frustrated that people I love dearly are disappointing me. And my reaction is to engage in shaming, maybe because I am hopeless to have things work out, to have things go better. Even though it feels like there's an ensnaring on my part going on, I, too, feel trapped in shame. So it cuts both ways. I find that in my family in particular this just feels like an unnecessarily bloody thing to do. But I feel like I do make more of an effort than the people around me to see where others are coming from. And when that isn't given to me, I can be extremely short-fused and hostile in my response."

Robbin recalled his father persistently making unfair demands of him in his youth, not accepting Robbin as he was, and trying to diminish Robbin for things that weren't his fault, looking for a place to take out his indignity when things didn't go his way. There were echoes of Robbin's father in the stories Robbin told of his interactions with Charles.

A particular trigger for Robbin was watching Charles persistently impose himself on Elsa. When Charles got physical with Elsa, the Shame Trapper rushed in, cued by Elsa not being seen, heard, and recognized. Robbin feared that her not being respected now would translate into her expectations for not being valued later in life. And lying beneath this valiant sense of rightness and justice was a projection of his own experience of not feeling seen, heard, and respected.

Robbin observed, "I think just seeing the inordinate and disproportionate level of crap that women put up with, and seeing Charles doling out that crap to someone who's two-and-a-half, just makes him a lightning rod for my rage. And I don't know how to approach it. Because on the one hand, I need to back off. And on the other hand, I want him to back off so much. Knowing the level of crap that Elsa is going to have to deal with simply for *being*, I don't want that to already start snowballing at age two. And it is."

"When I see this happening, I try to first calmly ask Charles to redirect his attention. But I have a pretty short fuse with it. So I shout. Yesterday, I can't even remember why I shouted, but I discussed it with him. And I told him afterwards, 'This is why I shouted. What can we do to make me not…?' I mean, even as I was saying that, it felt like I was engaging in some kind of shitty blackmail game. Like, *Can't help myself. What are you gonna do to make it so that I don't go there?* And it's like, what the fuck kind of parenting is that?"

"The Shame Trapper diminishes others, making them feel ashamed for what they're doing. It's a lot of blame. It often exists without a lot of work of setting expectations ahead of time, which I think can head the need for my shaming behavior off at the pass. So, in lieu of lots of boring, intellectual, heavy lifting on my part, it just shortcuts to taking no responsibility, feeling ashamed, spreading the feeling of shame, and just cutting people off at the knees."

Robbin reflected, "The Shame Trapper is super familiar because it feels like I'm channeling my dad all over again. But also a very bitter taste of this is not the me that I know that I'm capable of being. The being *trapped* in the name is so prominent for me. I feel trapped in the behavior. When Charles gets under my skin, my response is to want to trap him with shame. And that just seems so perverse. It's involuntary and dead wrong at the same time."

Though Robbin could locate the origins of the Shame Trapper and identify the unresolved trauma that cued this character onto the stage, he was in turmoil over owning that part of his father that he disliked so much as an aspect that was his, too. Robbin observed, "We like to force a lens of progress onto things, ourselves, our lives. And behaving in ways that remind us so starkly of our ancestors' palpably worst traits really flies in the face of that. And I think we resist that that's part of our composition."

Robbin coined a name for his characters that were cued onto the stage when he encountered the circumstances, the people, and the contexts that were reminiscent of these earlier stages in his development when the trauma first took root. He observed, "I've got what I'll call 'heirloom characters.' And it takes a lot to level with ourselves and with these characters and see them as part of the makeup, because we have another script running in our heads. *I should transcend this. I'm my own person.* I think some of our more grown-up characters carry conflicting messages about who we are supposed to be. And those limit how we can see ourselves, and which younger, more volatile characters we'll even acknowledge as being us."

Jennifer Garvey Berger identified parent-and-child relationships as those that are most genetically enmeshed and that have a tendency to call forth a younger self whose history and meaning is tied to an earlier identity. She mused, "The most primal relationships we have are with our parents and our kids. Those are ancient relationships; ancient in our lifespan, and also ancient in our mammalian progression. They bring up drives to protect at all costs. They have wandering and confusing overlapping identities. Genetically, they are us, and yet they're not us. I think there's some genetic pull that calls on us to be more enmeshed with those relationships."[1]

Robbin was enmeshed in both the genetic ancient relationships and the unresolved trauma that had taken root through them, and yet he pushed against that which held him and that which lived within him. Robbin struggled to try to love a father at the same time he felt repulsed by the way his father had gone through life. Over time, he began to accept the part of self that doesn't love a father the way one is "supposed to." And with reflection, he came to see that the Shame Trapper was a banished ghost of Robbin's theater of self that needed to be invited into the light.

Robbin said, 'I told the kids that I got shouted at a lot when I was a child. They asked why, and I said, 'Well, I think it was because my parents got shouted at a lot when they were children. And I'm really trying hard to not have it keep going this way.'

Heirloom characters are both aspects of self that we carry forward from those who came before us and parts of self that are shaped by our predecessor's story about who we are or who we should be. Our tendency to fight against these or to pull the curtain on them so that we might deny that they exist negates the presence of our full cast and the lessons they have to teach us. When we invite them into the light, we may be able to find compassion for them, and greater compassion for ourselves as complex beings carrying the weight of the stories imposed on us throughout our lifetime.

Perhaps development itself requires compromising aspects of self that are integral to the fullness of who we are. We have been coded upon by our elders, and we code upon our children, what we believe to be shameful and what is not. We teach them to deny parts of themselves that are essential to their whole being. How might we also allow them an outlet for that thing, an ability to bring it into the light of their full ensemble? One of the gifts of understanding fallback, particularly that which is precipitated by unresolved trauma, is that we may be able to unshackle those who follow from the weight of our traumas and constructed stories.

Over the past decade, I've been vexed by how to work with fallback triggered by trauma in my own explorations of fallback and in my accompaniment of others. This trigger for fallback and the depths to which it takes us has felt particularly challenging to confront, to establish a relationship with, to welcome into the cast and invite onto the stage with any sense that the character won't go rogue. What I have found is that, as with other triggers for fallback, we won't be able rid ourselves of the tether, but we can shift our relationship to it and employ tools to help us navigate it, integrate it, and learn from it.

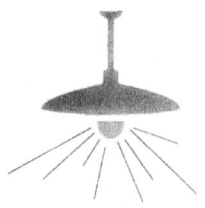

CHAPTER 13
YOUR TURN TO RECOGNIZE TRIGGERS

Flashback – Explore Your Character's Origin Story

Once we've come to recognize that there are many characters that make up our cast of self and begin to notice these fallback characters creeping onto the stage unintentionally, we can begin to more deeply explore our characters' origin stories. Reflecting on the scenes in which these characters have been prominent allows us to be honest with ourselves about how familiar our fallbacks are, what characters they tend to take the form of, what circumstances seem to beckon them, and what feels at risk. We come to know them better. We come to know the set better. We can see where the storyline is headed. And when these familiar characters—the usual suspects—come on stage, we can greet them accordingly. Hello, old friend. You've come again.

Watching the video reel of ourselves across context and over time allows us to see patterns. In this space, we may find language, perspective, recognition. We can also begin to determine if there is actually a threat to the value our characters are showing up in protection of. And if there is, we can begin to articulate, to self and others, what underlies our smaller characters' compulsion to storm the stage.

Exercise

Read through the scenes you identified and what you discovered for the character you selected at the end of chapter 10.

- Write down everything you fear, think, believe and assume in relation to the fallback experience you are focusing on. Everything. Unbridled and unedited. Write down all of the feelings of this experience, the beliefs, assumptions. Dig deep.

- Ask yourself what cued this character onto the stage? What felt at risk to you when this character came on the scene? What value is it protecting? What is triggering your fallback?

- Now, take every aspect of your self-talk in those moments of fallback and assess whether it is true, false, or you don't know.[1] In this way, we are able to loosen our grip on the assumptions we are making. We are able to determine if the part of self that is being beckoned on the scene is necessary, is reading from the right script, or if the lights need to come up to reveal to ourselves and others the storyline that underlies our characters' actions.

Once you have identified your triggers for fallback and have determined if there is indeed a threat, you are better equipped to articulate the value that feels threatened and to address it from that place…within self, in relationship to others. When we can articulate what our fallback is protecting in us, the thing that feels at risk and that is cueing the smaller versions of self onto the stage, we are better able to mitigate the damage that often ensues when our fallback characters storm the stage. What would happen in your conversations with those who experience you in fallback if you started from the place of, "This feels at risk to me. This is what this is about for me. And I see that [insert behavior in fallback] isn't the way to communicate this and connect with you. And I know that this is my default reaction. What this is really about for me is [insert what you value]."

CHAPTER 14
RECOVERING AND GROWING

While we often view our experiences of fallback as something we wish to reject, to flee from, there is a gift to be found in them. They point to something we value, something that feels at risk. Through our noticing and reflecting on the fallback experience, we are able to find the gift in fallback, find the value it is protecting, identify the ways in which all aspects of self, even the ones that we don't particularly like, do serve us so that we may recover and even grow. Paradoxically, while fallback is developmental decline in the moment, it can lead to growth when we shift our relationship to it.

Once we can see our fallback characters, come to know them, and befriend them, they don't feel so terrifying to us. We can begin to develop and cast costars that allow our characters to show up in their role in protection of us, but to do so in a way that doesn't thrash the props. We can practice the lines of a script that conveys our values in a way that doesn't present as a belligerent, incoherent monologue. We can construct a set that diminishes the need for our fallback characters to come on stage, because we've already tended in advance to the conditions and threats that may beckon them. We can even evaluate if the screenplay we have written is relevant for the times and conditions we are facing at this moment and decide to flip the script altogether.

But none of this is possible if we do not first show the courage to shine the light on the parts of self that are ever-present, that desire fiercely to act as our security force, protecting the aspects of life and self and other that we value. The process you've undertaken so far—identifying your fallback characters, articulating their origin stories, identifying the scenes in which they have shown up in your life, and understanding what it is that this part of us is trying to protect in us—is a step in the direction of recovery and growth.

And there are additional components necessary in allowing us to take the fallback that feels like decline in the moment and letting the gift of healing and growth emerge. Integral to our recovery and growth from fallback is becoming clear about our intentions for the acts and scenes of our lives and bridging the gap between those intentions and how we are actually showing up. We must shift the narrative about our inevitable experiences of fallback to frame those times we miss our lines or trip over the props as opportunities to try again, to practice, to learn, to grow. We will need to embrace all parts of self, the bigness and the smallness, recognizing that it is the integration of our full ensemble that allows us to live into the messy, beautiful wholeness of self and from that space to have greater choice, a broader repertoire of how we show up, and greater connection to the full story of our lives and our becoming. And we will need to practice acceptance and love for the fullness of self.

Intention

In every single one of our relationships, in every context, in every interaction, we likely have implicit intentions, a way that we hope to show up and a longed-for outcome. For most of us, this intention goes unspoken, perhaps not even held prominently outside of our subconscious minds. We must bring our intentions into the light.

Intention is an incredibly powerful anchor. It provides a frame through which to notice that the character that we are showing up as may be a far cry from who we wish to be. It is in this gap that awareness may be cultivated. Intention offers a touchstone against which we can hold our values and measure whether we are engaging in the world in a way that aligns with them.

David McCallum suggested, "The relationship to our fallback opens up a space for us to think about *how is this aligned with my values and the value I want to contribute in this moment?* And to have that stance of inquiry about *what is it that I care about? Who is it that I care about? Why? And how does that lead and guide me to want to offer something in this moment?* All those things for me are expressions of that relational space between the instant and our actions."[1] Indeed, when we become clear about our intentions, we are able to tap into the true essence and desires of the self.

In the beginning, Robbin was only really cognizant of the outsized performances of the Turf Roarer and the Shame Trapper. The bit part performances had historically gone unnoticed. But once he began to explore his cast of characters in depth and hold their performances up against the lines of the script he desired to write and the intentions he had for his relationship with his family, he noticed the impact of these characters' appearances. Robbin observed, "I'm coming to recognize the damage of the habitual behavior. I'm not blind to how every time those characters come out, I'm poorer for it, not to mention everybody else. I've come to realize that my behavior always feels unnecessary and ineluctable. That's the fallback right there. Watching yourself be a shithead in real time."

McCallum suggested getting to the balcony about our mental processes by taking a meta-view on them—checking in with the heart, paying attention to our desires—giving us more freedom to make sense and act differently.[2] An awareness of fallback can help increase our options for how we show up and set explicit intentions for our interactions.

Connecting with our intentions can also help us identify what characters we may need to develop to serve as helpful accompanying costars to the fallback characters that are often cast on the scene. While our fallback characters may steal the stage and thrash the set when they are cast as a solo act, they are often able to find greater nuance and finesse when they dance with other characters, some of whom may only be in the early stages of discovery and development. At first, the lines that these more graceful characters read may be only a mantra, serving as a reminder of the intention that they are aligned with. Over time and with practice, we are able to offer our grace characters a broader repertoire of actions.

Robbin began to consider the tired role that he repeatedly played in his interactions with Charles over the protection of physical turf and to evaluate its effectiveness in allowing him to form the relationship that he so desired with his children. Robbin noted, "Sometimes I really do need to make sure that no one is trying to sit on joints and force them to go the other way. But I can also recognize when I'm reacting with physical revulsion to someone coming up to me when I don't want it that I need to shift gears immediately and be kind of a Mushy Hug Monster. And that takes something. But it's an extra layer of intelligence saying, *The reaction that's on tap is not called for and runs counter to a bigger commitment. You have a finite number of interactions with your kids. You don't need to blow them on default reactions and have those be the defining interactions. You have what it takes to correct course. Now do that.*"

The Mushy Hug Monster was not an established character in Robbin's repertoire. But Robbin could see the need to develop him, and he began to cast him alongside the Turf Roarer and the Shame Trapper. The role of the Turf Roarer was to protect the physical boundaries and safety of the actors on the stage. The role of the Shame Trapper was to assess when actions threatened to disrespect another's capacity to be seen, heard, and respected. And the role of the Mushy Hug Monster was to direct the action away from the threats and toward the intentions of building loving relationships through light-hearted and fun interactions with and between Robbin's children.

When we notice that we are in fallback, when we recognize the gap between our intentions for who we wish to be and how we are showing up, when we name it, at least within self, it's a clue to pause. Pause and connect to intention. Pause and step away from the person with whom we are in conflict. Pause and reflect on what we are grateful for. Pause and take a breath, and then another, and then another. Pause and become a Mushy Hug Monster. In the pause prompted by noticing the gap between action and intention, we gain greater choice for how we may proceed. Even if the choices don't open up in the moment, noticing that we are in fallback beckons us to reflection after action, and in this reflection new possibilities emerge. We need to mind the gap between our intentions and our reality, our espoused values versus our values in use.[3] These can serve as a North Star to guide us to our bigger self.

Indeed, when we come to know the script that is playing in the mind, we become aware of the lines as they are being read and may be able to determine if the narrative needs a rewrite. The intellect—the rational, knowing mind that is often at the forefront of ego, identity, and self-protection—can be a powerful tool in recovering from fallback when not used in isolation.

Narrative

As we develop our capacity to notice and come to know the characters that make up our ensemble, as we become aware of the truth of our experience and when we are showing up in the gap between our intentions and something far less aligned with them, recovery out of our smaller self begins to happen more quickly.

Yet awareness of our fallback and the gap between it and our intentions, while integral to our recovery and growth, is only one factor. Narrative is another. The narratives that pervade our environment have significant implications for how we understand our capacity to show up in the world in the best conditions and how we deal with our inevitable encounters with the worst.

An understanding of the importance of narrative in our experience of fallback is a pivotal aspect of its outcome, positive or negative.[4] The stories we tell ourselves are created with and from our context. It is not only our self narrative but the narrative of our surround, our relationships, our organizations, our society and culture that puts the possibility of recovery and growth right in front of us…or does not.

McCallum suggested that framing fallback as an indication that some positive growth is on the horizon is helpful in both recovery and learning from fallback. He explained, "We make mistakes, and we do things that we regret. And from a religious perspective, we sin. One way of thinking about sin is from the Greek *hamartia*, to miss the mark. I've missed the mark, and now I'm going to learn and figure out how to hit the mark the next time. That's really healthy and adaptive as a stance toward life."[5]

Berger claimed, "It is normal that we dip into these places. It's not wrong or bad. It feels like what it is to be alive. And what it is to be alive is to stretch into the full range of our humanness, the full range of our development."[6]

Facing our fallback with the intent to invite it in, to come face-to-face with the aspect of self or the value that it is protecting and learn from it, allows us to see fallback for the gift it is. It provides a recognition that the full, messy, complexity is part of us, too. To recover from fallback, to grow, requires us to acknowledge that fallback makes us human, and we can learn to appreciate it, us, all of us. It is a paradox that suffering can lead to insight when we make the choice to turn shame and regret into gratitude.

One aspect of the positive framing of fallback is knowing that we are not alone in our experience of showing up in our smaller self. We are not the only ones who miss the mark. And there will come a time when we will hit the mark. Jennifer Garvey Berger recalled telling her son in his moments of fallback, "I want you to know, everybody feels this way. This way that you are feeling, it's a momentary feeling. I don't know whether it's going to last a little while or a long time. But there is this now, and then there is something else that comes after now. This is a moment. When you lose yourself, you are going to find yourself again. When you're in your small self, big self is not gone. It's just not with you right at that moment."[7]

I say this to my children now. I say this to myself when I feel in the depths of my despair, unable to access the part of me that I know has different ways of showing up but to which I can't gain access. And it gives me hope.

Sometimes the wisdom in narrative form comes not from our parents, as it did for Jennifer's son, but from our children.

"I am alive." My friend Gideon's toddler daughter has taken to proclaiming this regularly, randomly. What a reminder it is to notice the thing we probably most take for granted. We breathe, infusing our blood with oxygen. Our hearts beat, pumping this oxygen-infused blood through our bodies, nourishing our organs. Our brains send signals to our limbs, and our nerves return communication to our brains.

I am alive.

I am alive is something we forget in the moments when fallback has us crashing down onto the rocky and sandy shoreline. We struggle mightily, thinking that the effort will allow us to find safe land. The abrasion of our smaller self scratches, pokes, stings, mars. Or perhaps it is merely exfoliating. Rubbing away the dead skin that no longer serves us. Surfacing the new, the tender, the raw. Reminding ourselves that *I am alive* and that the scrapes we feel are a call to discover the values that we hold most dear allows us to reframe our experiences of fallback from something we are fighting against to something we would do well to embrace.

Integration

When we are in our smaller, more shadowy periods of fallback, we begin to think that we're not human. We demonize ourselves, which leads to the shame and blame and rejection of that part of self. Conveniently, we forget that a smaller self even came on the scene, is even part of our ensemble, until it inevitably shows up in the theater again.

Robbin observed, "It's almost like amnesia. I tend to avoid parts that don't align with my constructed self-image. And the funny thing is that they're stock characters. They reliably come back. And it's like the director doesn't have them on the payroll, which probably ensures that they come back. *Where's my pay, goddammit?!*"

One of the choices we have when we find ourselves in fallback is how we will respond to seeing ourselves in this way, in our smallness. Often, our initial reaction is to deflect responsibility, to blame the way we are showing up on others, on the circumstance, on the context. In those cases, when we come through our fallback, we believe that we are all fixed, because what precipitated the fallback is *out there*. That part of self doesn't live in us, it just made a fleeting guest appearance.

That's not how it works. All of our characters, all parts of self, will always live within us. If we don't acknowledge them, if we don't give them credit for their past performances, if we don't keep a watchful eye on when they may be prompted to make their next appearance, they cannot be of use to us. They cannot be of use to anyone else.

"I think there's an interesting set of questions about what fallback enables, in terms of what its gifts and possibilities are for how we can see ourselves, and then that seeing ourselves actually becomes a springboard to a bigger self," noted Berger. "What does knowing about it offer my development? What does looking for it offer my development?"[8]

As Berger suggests, one's development, either expanding or shrinking, can be influenced by one's relationship to fallback.[9] Indeed, fallback has the capacity to lead to a virtuous cycle of growth. But it may also result in a vicious cycle of decline. Which way it goes may be closely correlated with one's developmental stage and one's relationship to fallback.

Our willingness to recognize and own a part of self that is not what we wish to project increases as we open the rooms in our developmental house. When we have a relationship to fallback that allows us to take responsibility, we have access to options to respond differently. Yet, at any developmental stage, we can work to cultivate the capacity for integration of our full self.

That whole ideal of perfection, the identity we fiercely defend that we have never had a bad thought or action, that we are fully in control—that's not real. There's something powerful about reframing being human from being a perfect human to being a full human, rich with complexity and messiness.

As Robbin reflected on his experiences of fallback, he began to claim all of these parts of self. "The ways that I've come up with to be in family and to love have primarily constituted a denial of my dad's behaviors. And I guess there's some arrogance in that, that something that feels beyond my control, that I feel subject to, is trying to override. Like if I'm going to be, I need to be all of it. And I can't just pick and choose the dainty pieces that I would select."

An understanding of which characters are called onto the stage and why can facilitate decision-making in action. If we can reframe why we are acting from an earlier stage of development from a developmental perspective, we are no longer subject to the action. It is fallback until one is able to put a new frame of choice around the behavior. An awareness of fallback can help expand our options for how we show up and allow us to set explicit intentions for our interactions. Coming into relationship with our fallback and the characters that inhabit it gives us more freedom and opens up new possibilities.

It is only through embracing the full self, shadowy bits included, that we gain access to the lessons that fallback can offer. Fallback invites us to inquire into the truth of our assumptions about the way things are and about the way we are in relationship to them. It encourages our awareness of the full ensemble of self and what each of the characters is in protection of. It invites us to articulate our fears and face into them with compassion and acceptance rather than looking for the nearest trap door or burning down the set. Fallback beckons us to notice which characters are performing in the scenes of our lives and how familiar the patterns are, and to become more intentional about casting from our full ensemble, rather than calling in the usual suspects.

Integration of the full cast of our characters requires that we first acknowledge that they exist within the ensemble of self. Then we can invite them onto the stage, into the illumination of the ghost light, and walk around them, examine them, request that they share their gifts. Over time, we will become more comfortable with claiming the full stable of self as something that is not out there at a distance, but part of us. We come to recognize that yes, indeed, we do sometimes fallback. And sometimes these characters help us grow. We step into a spacious place of holding and accepting the full cast when they show up, and we begin to consider how we might work with them more effectively.

Acceptance

Perhaps the most important step in recovery and growth is to accept the fallback as us, as a part of self that is not going away. Because here's the thing—I don't think you cure this. But in coming to know what these parts of ourselves represent, and what value feels threatened that beckons these characters onto the stage, we come to know the fullness of self better, the whole kit and kaboodle of our complexity and richness. I'm not offering an antidote to eradicate fallback from your life. I'm inviting you into a different relationship with it. Because it will always be with you and that, in fact, is a gift.

Our own acceptance of our full self is mightily aided when others can see the fullness of us and love us just the same. In fact, we often find that they love us more for our willingness to claim the messiness, the darkness and the light, of what it is to be human—a darkness and light that lives in them, too. Acceptance by others of our smallest self is a powerful catalyst for recovery from fallback.

If we're fortunate, like Diego, we may have someone who can help us identify what we are sometimes unable to see by ourselves. Diego recalled, "Kyra encouraged me to not see all of this as a disease or a sin or something broken, but to see it as a new way of making sense of myself. She helped me see how those pieces of myself that I was self-loathing were actually essential for the parts of myself that were important and attractive and effective in the world." Having the opportunity to see through another's lens is powerful. It's even more powerful when that lens is permeated with love and acceptance of the whole of us, warts and all.

Diego continued to experience the gift of acceptance as he owned his truth, sharing the full messiness of the various parts of himself with others. One friend and colleague, having heard his story said, "I love you more for it. You are more human to me, having described this." Diego recalled, "That sealed the moment when I said okay, I am not a monster. And now that I'm aware of this stuff, I can start dealing with it."

The fact that others were able to accept Diego's full self, loving the parts of him that he feared were unlovable, allowed Diego to accept himself. Acceptance opened the road to recovery from fallback. Seeing the mechanism of fallback, analyzing what happened and understanding what felt at risk to him, moved Diego further along the path. Intention, in this case related to his role in a love relationship, provided the motivation to show up better, because he had something, someone, worth working for.

Over time, and with purpose, Diego was able to move more smoothly between the different parts of himself. There's the aspect that defends boundaries about what it means to win, to be safe and in control. Then there's the part that can project love, kindness, and generosity. Diego found that he was able to hold both, bringing the two parts together almost in the same sentence, in the same moment, as opposed to snapping. "Once I understood the mechanism and accepted that it's part of me, I wasn't going to reject it, saying it's bad and dump it. See, if it's part of me, it's a resource. I should be able to use it without being hijacked by it."

We don't ever get rid of our fallback. And we don't want to. Because coming into relationship with the full ensemble of our characters, leaving the ghost light on to illuminate them, allows us to be intentional and strategic about which characters show up and how they move together so that we may act in accordance with who we want to be in a situation, who we want to be in the world. When we lose access to what our fallback is trying to teach us, we lose a vital, integral part of who we are, a protective mechanism that reminds us that we are human. When we trust in the wisdom of the fullness of ourselves, realizing that it is all us, we are able to grow.

Growth

Even as we build our capacity from reflecting on our fallback after the fact, to being able to witness it as it's happening, to being able to do something about it in the moment or soon after, to being able to anticipate its arrival, we will fall back. And we also have the capacity to spring forward, to learn and grow from our fallback, from the characters that take us to that smaller part of self, because they take us there with a purpose, with a message, if we are willing to listen to it and turn on the ghost light within self.

In order to grow from fallback, instead of pushing our smaller self away in disgust, yelling, "Get this off of me!" we need to embrace it all. We need to invite the spirits of self to share their knowledge. Once we understand the lesson they are there to teach, our goal is not to then lock them backstage. Instead, we can cast them in the scenes of our lives with intention, with helpful costars, with a script and direction that allows them to portray what we value in a way that is not so harmful and destructive. And once all of the characters of self are not banished but can take their rightful places on stage, they are able to bring their knowledge as gifts rather than the kind of storming-the-stage-before-falling-in-the-pit that has marked their appearances heretofore.

Yet it is important to realize that development doesn't happen in an instant, and it is not all onward and upward, sweetness and light. To think that you have this problem once, you do a little bit of work to address it, and then you're just going to move along past it is not realistic.

An understanding of fallback challenges us to make those experiences of fallback learning experiences. It encourages both a long-term view of development and a moment-to-moment awareness. The latter to remind us that development is a process, work that must be undertaken throughout one's life. The former for forgiveness and hope. An understanding of fallback allows us to have hope in the work.[10]

Chuck Palus, reflecting on the teachings of one of the pioneers of developmental theory, Erik Erikson, recalled, "Erikson was talking about the idea of *forever adolescing*. That at each stage of our lives, we are revisiting the earlier tasks. We don't just stride through them and finish them. That life is a tapestry. The whole tapestry idea is that, wherever you are, you're ideally in touch with the tasks that you thought you had passed, but actually they keep being reminded at each stage. So, the forever adolescing, I take it as something to do with identity. We're always reforming our identities and recrafting our identities. And if you think you've finished with that work, it's never finished. And every new stage of life almost compels you to go through the tapestry again and revisit the stages. And so it's much more of a looping and recycling than it is a ladder. Wherever you are in your life cycle, you are in touch, and you better be working on the things you thought you finished. And that's the real work of life, not just sort of checking the boxes and becoming more aware."[11]

Development is not a destination to arrive at, but an ongoing journey with ever cycling opportunities to come to know self more fully and authentically, more chances to integrate that which has been left unresolved.

One of the gifts of fallback is that it jolts us out of our complacency about how development happens and our hubris at having arrived. There is no arrival. The journey is ongoing. Fallback provides the invitation to venture ever more deeply into the yet-to-be discovered and understood to a deeper, more nuanced, more truthful relationship with self. Fallback offers a window to our blind spots.[12]

My goal in illuminating fallback is not to see it so it can be rejected, but to see it so it can be embraced. *This*, too, is me. And giving attention to *this*, naming *this*, may help me and others expand our range of options not only for how we make meaning or show up or exist in relationship with others, but for how we enter into relationship with self…more authentically…more whole.[13]

CHAPTER 15
OCTAVIA RECOVERING AND GROWING

We first met Octavia in the grip of her fallback with her new division director, Brenda. After the fallback, she could see that there were other ways she could have engaged, that she wished that she had, but in the moment she was unable to access those capacities. In the period following her fallback, there was much that Octavia regretted about the way she had shown up in her interactions with Brenda, in her integrity to herself. Her experiences of fallback and her commitment to reflecting on them, to coming to understand the characters that entered the scene and what they were coming in protection of, revealed patterns of fallback in other contexts of her life and revealed other characters, each with an aspect of self that they were in service to.

Over the years, Octavia got better at recovering from her episodes of fallback and doing so closer to the moment of their occurrence. She was able to articulate her fears and locate their origins in her history. She began to question the truth of the assumptions that she had made. She could see the gift in her fallback characters, the ways that they served her, and how she might begin to cast and direct them together in the scenes of her life.

Octavia named her intentions, tapping into the true essence and desires of self that her fallback revealed. She worked deliberately to cultivate the characters that would allow her to meet these. At the same time, Octavia would grow in relationship to her characters, both big and small, embracing them for the full, authentic humanness that they offered as she came to better know her self. Octavia moved with purpose into the contexts that invited her developing characters to be present, that would allow them to rehearse their parts, hone their craft. All the while she learned to acknowledge and accept the characters that represented smaller aspects of herself for the gifts that they, too, offered.

In the pages that follow, we will come to know the full ensemble of characters that made up Octavia's theater of self. We will witness how Octavia's developmental decline in her moments of fallback transformed into deep learning, acceptance, recovery, and growth.

The Expert

A wave of shame washed over Octavia as Brenda decried her handling of the video project in a room full of Octavia's peers. She felt incompetent. At least she felt it was Brenda's intent to paint her as incompetent. Yet in the moment of fallback, she was having a hard time not internalizing the incompetence that Brenda projected upon her. Octavia was struggling not to question herself.

Attempting to save face, Octavia's Expert marched onto the stage. Octavia recalled, "I was trying to explain things to Brenda, which was frustrating, because I felt like she was not open to hearing them at all. There were points where I may have seemed defensive around it."

Octavia knew herself to be both credible and competent, but with Brenda's public shaming, Octavia's identity was challenged. *Was Brenda right? Was this a failure?* For a time, Octavia was unable to recognize the capable professional she knew herself to be. And in doubting herself, Octavia felt as if she had let herself down.

What's more, though the projects Brenda was critiquing were Octavia's, Brenda wouldn't even look at her, would not address her directly, and seemed unwilling to recognize the capabilities and credentials that had earned Octavia this role to begin with. Another blow to Octavia's identity was struck as she felt her personhood was not respected.

Octavia began to realize her concerns about credibility and competence masked a deeper threat to her sense of being respected—her need for autonomy and control and her quest for freedom. Octavia wanted to flee.

The Unprotected Little

Brenda's unilateral approach, her closed-offness, her attachment to a narrow and incomplete view, reminded Octavia of circumstances of her youth where she felt unsafe. The Unprotected Little came on the scene beckoned by the unresolved trauma that Brenda's exercise of "power-over" was reminiscent of.

Octavia observed, "The Unprotected Little is a very young part of myself. It comes from an early childhood space. And so, when I get into that fearful space, that's the part that gets triggered, these survival fears."

Octavia wanted to quit. She remembered, "I told myself *you are not quitting. This is so ridiculous.* But I knew I was in a bad space when I had that thought because that is so important to me to be able to keep myself safe and to determine what environments are going to be conducive for my flourishing and safety. Brenda's approach was an affront to that. And usually when I want to escape something, it is because my sense of freedom feels threatened."

This was not a one-off issue with Brenda or a part of Octavia that was only present in the work environment. Later, Octavia would come to identify multiple contexts, both professional and personal, in which she located the fire escape because her sense of freedom and security was challenged. Octavia observed, "When you have these insights, they continue to work on you in different ways. There is a way where I'm bringing that insight into my other spheres, especially the relational spheres."

Octavia had been in a romantic relationship with a man, Reese, for several months. She was drawn to him on an energetic and spiritual level. She felt there was something they were meant to learn from each other. Yet she was under no illusion that their relationship was headed to the altar. Octavia longed to be in a relationship with someone who could hold space for her, could see her, who was willing to effort through the self- and relational experience to be in mutuality and inquiry with her. And she was clear that Reese was not this person.

Yet Reese was looking for assurances that their relationship was headed for something stable, long term. As he continued to push for her to make promises beyond her desires, Octavia began to feel powerless, like she was unable to influence the situation. Old fears came into play. *What if I let my guard down and I am proven right—that another can't hold me? Will I still be able to protect myself? If I commit to another, what do I give up about myself?*

Beckoned by the unresolved trauma of not having her needs met by another person as a child or in adulthood, the Unprotected Little stumbled onto the scene and exclaimed, "Fuck this shit. I'm out of here."

Octavia observed, "If I feel like I can't influence the situation, it becomes very challenging for me. I want to go. I am a committed person, on the one hand. And then there's a part of me that always needs to have an escape hatch. I normally don't cut and run, but I have a strong desire to. I stay in this space of ambivalence."

Octavia could see the ways in which the Unprotected Little served her. "In the past my instinct to flee has been self-protective because my other relationships have been very toxic," Octavia reflected. "So it is actually wisdom for me to get the hell out of here. I think that is where the desire to not repeat some of those things comes from. I do want to make sure that I'm making good decisions for myself, that I'm not getting myself into this pattern of unhealthy relationships with people who are not well-matched to me. I guess I have not been able to figure out how to do that."

The relationships that were *supposed* to have offered Octavia stability, safety, and protection had not done so historically. At a very young age, Octavia discovered that she could only depend on herself. Whenever her agency to do so was threatened, she had a strong protective impulse to flee. Octavia observed, "Some of it is making sure that I don't get hurt. That's the main thing, that I am responsible for protecting myself. That I cannot really expect or trust other people to protect me. So, I have to be vigilant around that."

Octavia and I began exploring her experiences of fallback years before we commenced methodically identifying scenes and characters. When we did begin to shine the ghost light on Octavia's characters using theater as a metaphor, much had changed in the material manifestations of her life. She had moved to a different state, taken a new job at an organization that was much more aligned with her soul's yearning, and resumed an international long-distance relationship with a man whom she had known for half her life.

Octavia and Cornell had been in each other's lives for decades, sometimes romantically, sometimes just as friends, always in love. They had decided to give their romantic relationship another go, hoping that the stars would align on the circumstances of their lives this time, allowing the material aspects of their relationship to come into flow.

Working to maintain closeness and connection across an international relationship had not been an easy undertaking. It became much more difficult when the pandemic hit and the world shut down. After six months of separation, Octavia was at last able to visit Cornell for an extended period of time. She knew it would be a crucible moment in their relationship and hoped the stage would be set for meaningful decisions to be made about their future.

In her freewrite, Octavia wrote:

I'm visiting Cornell, and I'm freaking out. I'm outside of myself in my life, in someone else's. Trying to be good, appear good. I notice myself in a familiar pattern over-efforting and performing and taking care of someone else's needs above my own. What am I doing here in this space yet again? Why am I doing this? I feel like I have to cover up these messy feelings and emotions, protect Cornell from me, not make waves or upset him. I feel stuck and in a bind between my relationship to this man and beloved and my relationship with myself. I feel insecure and dispossessed. How can I choose myself?

I desire to show up fully as my whole and authentic self and in relationship. But the gap is that I am hiding myself, betraying myself to get love and approval, to be good and to be seen as good.

Through the process of viewing the playback screen of her life, Octavia identified the Unprotected Little, the Good Girl, the Woman, and the Sorceress.

The Unprotected Little - Reprise

Unlike Octavia's relationship with Reese, a deep soul connection bonded she and Cornell, a love that had spanned their own becoming as individuals and their coming anew into relationship. But as in her relationship with Reese, Octavia felt that Cornell was unable to hold and take care of her in the way she desired to be held, in the way she needed to be cared for in order to feel safe. During this visit he continued to demonstrate through his non-initiative that this was true.

Cornell resisted engaging in the tough conversations about their relationship and the logistics of how to keep it thriving over the long distance and time. Octavia explained to Cornell, "I can't rely on you to make and keep commitments to me and *us* in our relationship. Because you can't even have a planning conversation around when we will next see each other. Even if it's something that's not possible or you might have to make some sacrifices, that's what we do, right? We make goals. And then we try to figure out how to make them happen. And when you're not making that kind of effort for me or our relationship, it doesn't make me feel like you're trying to take care of me. Everything that happens in our relationship happens because I'm planning it or pushing it forward. And I don't want to be in that kind of relationship. We're both adults. When I'm not in a great space or a generous space, I can tell myself stories that maybe you aren't as committed to the relationship."

Octavia noted, "That's what was happening in that relationship with Reese. And with Cornell, I sometimes feel like he doesn't quite have his shit together enough, so I have to step into the gap. And because he has to tend to his own priorities, there's not enough extra to focus on me either. It feels like I'm not being taken care of."

Once again, Octavia's sense of safety, security, and desire to be held and to be cared for was at risk. Octavia, having identified the Unprotected Little in her relationship with Reese, was catching herself in a pattern of giving too much with nothing in return. In reaction to what she perceived as a lack of commitment and effort on Cornell's part, Octavia became resentful, and the familiar ambivalence kicked in about whether Cornell was even the right person for her. Her desire to escape took hold. Yet Octavia had developed her ability to articulate her fears both to herself and to others and hold steady rather than catching the next flight out when she had a desire to flee. Besides, the Unprotected Little was not the only character in the scenes of her relationship with Cornell.

The Good Girl

Enter the Good Girl. Octavia revealed, "The Good Girl wants to be perfect, and do everything right, and be seen as good, and not have any negative emotions that upset anybody. The Good Girl can hold everything, is needless and wantless in many ways. She's the way that I wish to be seen." Octavia refers to this part of self as "Easy Breezy Cover Girl," and she has been hanging around the stage of her relationships since Octavia was a child.

Unresolved trauma set the stage for the Good Girl coming on the scene. As a preteen, Octavia adored her mother but felt neglected by her. Octavia justified her mother's behavior, negating her own feelings and desires in order to take on her mother's perspective. Octavia recalled, "I learned early on that your intimate people *don't* meet your needs. That's the genesis of my Good Girl. You won't have your needs met, so it's better to not have any needs."

Octavia noted, "When others don't take care of business, my caretaking and hyper-responsibility emerges. I fill in the gap rather than withdraw my energy from the situation because that's how I gained love and value when I was younger. I do things, and I give, and I produce in hopes that somehow that translates into me receiving the love that I want from people. And what I have learned over the years is that is not how that works. You don't get the love that you give to people. You get the love that people have to give you. And you don't earn it. People just give what they have to give and what they want to give. And that is such a hard kind of wiring to undo and sit with. What I resent the most about it is that it triggers that response of me over-efforting to fill in the gaps."

This script of how Octavia gets loved played on repeat in her relationships. "I am clear that I do manifest these relationships. I feel like I am dating versions of my mother over and over again. I attract and also subconsciously feel attracted to people who need me in a certain way. And I have a lot of capacity to hold. So I play out this family psychodrama around holding and how I can't be held."

Octavia observed, "The Good Girl is part of how the people I love and care about feel loved or cared for by me. It's the Good Daughter or the Good Girlfriend. I'm anticipating what their needs are. I'm engaged with them. The people who are in close relationship to me love it because they feel held and seen and taken care of." The Good Girl without a doubt served the needs of others.

But Octavia was getting something out of the Good Girl's presence, as well. Octavia admitted, "It's not that the Good Girl is not me, either. I do feel like I have a caretaking personality. And I genuinely like to take care of the people I love." There's a rush when the Good Girl comes on stage. It feels nice. The Good Girl keeps the peace and preserves relationships. When the Good Girl is on the scene, Octavia doesn't fear being seen or seeing self as unworthy, she doesn't have to reveal her messy parts to others, she won't be rejected.

But the Good Girl also takes a toll. When she comes on stage, Octavia feels performative, as if she is in a dream state. She observed, "In my relationships, the Good Girl fundamentally doesn't serve me, because I'm not able to get my needs met. It also reinforces this idea that I'm not worthy of love and care as I am. Because, if I perceive that I get the love that I want through this character, I don't get to see what kind of holding I can get if I'm in my full beauty and messiness. And so that is not serving my intentions of showing up fully and authentically in relationship in a way where I can be taken care of. The Good Girl doesn't allow me to be taken care of."

This is how the script is written for us. And once we are typecast in a given role, in Octavia's case as the Good Girl, it's hard to break out of that role. It's difficult for others to accept us and for us to accept ourselves without judgment or shame or embarrassment as we attempt to deviate from the lines on the paper.

Indeed, there's a way in which we collude in the typecasting of self. We sometimes set people up to fail, to not serve our needs, because we put this false version of who we are into the world. We do not show our full vulnerabilities and messiness and complexity. Then the audience is shocked when we do let the less-pristine aspects of self peek out from behind the curtain. And because others are accustomed to us showing up in a certain way that indicates we seemingly have it all together, they may offer us less grace when we clearly don't. And they certainly don't rise up to meet the needs that we've been trying like hell not to show them we have. We are often accomplices in others' expectations of us.

Octavia could see the value in integrating even her smaller characters. "I think that's why it's important. The intention is to show up as full and whole—*not* perfect. Because then you don't even set up that expectation from people," observed Octavia. "I have really thought about this a lot over the years around how I'm complicit in not getting my own needs met. People don't perceive that I have needs because I don't show them. I look like I have everything together. I'm the responsible one. I'm the one who knows. People come to me."

The Good Girl is not only triggered by the unresolved trauma of not having her needs met by those who *should* have met her needs as a child. The Good Girl has become part of the identity that Octavia has constructed in order to not have her security hijacked and her psychological self shattered. The Good Girl exists so she can be seen and see herself as someone who is worthy of love. She invites the self-fulfilling prophecy, *I am not worthy of love if I'm not minimizing my perspective, wants, and needs. I will not ever find someone who can meet my wants and needs.* Octavia was trying to come to terms with how she could draw a line around how much she was willing to give to others and still be "good."

Throughout her life, Octavia had continued to write the same script with the same characters. She had heretofore been unable to flip the script to invite new cast members in, her own and others', to see if some new plot might emerge. But with time and as she connected to her intention, it felt like something was shifting.

Octavia reflected, "I genuinely do want to be of service to the people I love and care about. I don't want my mom to be suffering. I don't want Cornell to be suffering. I do want to help them. But then I just can't sometimes. And I think leaving people to their own devices is a boundary that I'm trying to work with in some ways. And it doesn't mean that I'm not kind, or I'm not a good daughter, or I'm not all these other things. I think one of my desires of late, which is connected to this commitment to myself, is to be in relationship with people where it's mutual. That really is my guiding star. And when I catch myself in this pattern, which is very familiar, to escape from it."

The Woman

There was a confluence of characters on the scene in Octavia's interactions with Cornell. There was the Unprotected Little who, sensing Octavia's security, freedom, power, and agency were at risk, prepared to flee. The Good Girl, persistent and earnest in her desire to make the relationship work, pretended not to have needs or desires for fear of discovering that her partner can't tend to them. And then there was the Woman, holding herself in integrity around not just being of service to another but expecting mutuality.

The scenes of Octavia's life where the Woman was cast alongside the Good Girl and the Unprotected Little were many, though the Woman was just beginning to come into view in her intimate relationships like the one with Reese three years prior. At the time she observed, "Part of what Reese likes about me is the shininess of me, for lack of a better way to say it. There's a way that I'm a catalyst for growth for a lot of the men that I end up in relationship with. I find that problematic. Who's catalyzing my growth? Or am I just solely in service to these men who feel like they've had this transformative experience of themselves being in relationship to me? That does me no fucking good. I'm happy for you, that you're having this transformative experience at the cost of me, basically. So I had this twinge of *I'm not here to grow you* with Reese."

Octavia continued, "It's protection, and it is also integrity, too. My goal in this intimate relationship is to feel like I'm meeting this personal standard and value of mine that I have set—my integrity. There's a part of me that feels like I have to hold myself accountable to having my needs met. Especially since I have such a history of getting into bad relationships with people, not repeating these patterns."

In Octavia's relationship with Reese, she had created an explicit intention of prioritizing her own needs and staying true to them. She grabbed onto that intention like a beacon, determined to stay in integrity to this self that she was creating who isn't dependent on another to meet her needs and who isn't being used to meet theirs. The burgeoning Woman adopted a mantra: "I'm not here to grow you," as she worked to choose herself over her relationships with others.

However, when Octavia chooses Octavia, it's not just being in integrity to herself, it is choosing the path of security. The Woman knows that she can provide for herself, including the basic needs that haven't been met by others. Though the Woman is willing to walk away, she first establishes boundaries and makes her values known.

"The Woman has only come out more recently in my relationships as I've tried to get clearer about what my needs are and to articulate them. I've allowed myself to express those needs more, and sometimes that expression comes out as a demand or in outbursts. But not that often. Because I think, again, this Good Girl needless and wantless energy is very strong and powerful."

Octavia explained, "I feel like the Woman and the Good Girl get into fights with each other. They're kind of warring characters. I talk myself out of my own needs, desires, and feelings because I take other people's perspectives. It feels like a form of gaslighting. The Good Girl gaslights the Woman."

Indeed, the Good Girl and the Woman often are cast in the same scene, fighting for the lead. Octavia noted, "In the moment of conflict with Cornell, I would allow myself to be angry. Before, whenever those things would happen, I would shut it down. But I have that self-talk. 'You need to communicate calmly and in a way that people can hear.' That's that Good Girl reasoning. The Woman responds, 'No, that's bullshit. There's nothing wrong with being angry. You're angry. And you can show that you're angry. It's natural.'"

With awareness of the familiar patterns and the roles each of her characters were called on stage to play, Octavia began to inquire into the truth of her assumptions, particularly in the context of her relationship with Cornell. She wondered, "Is it something I need to give myself? Or is it something that I need somebody else to give to me? It shouldn't be this binary. And it's probably a little bit of both. I do feel like I am giving more. Maybe not more than what I want to be giving, because I do like giving. But I don't want to be giving and not receiving anything, either. That's the mutuality part. Before, it took me forever to be able to say that. Because it sounds like that's not something that we should say. But then I think, what is shameful about me saying that I want something from people? That's this hyper-independence around not needing people."

Octavia recounted conversations she had with Cornell when the Woman came on the scene, articulating her values and drawing boundaries to protect them from being disregarded. She told Cornell, "Look, I want to feel protected by you and safe in this relationship. And there are specific reasons why I don't feel that. Part of what makes me not feel that in a relationship, not just in this one, is if I have to be the one giving so much. Because that sends a signal to me that this person needs me. And they are not stepping up to take care of themselves, and/or they are not taking care of me either. My desire to be held feels threatened when I'm the only one efforting or planning or doing anything tangible to show the commitment to the other. But also a desire for me to keep my own commitments to myself."

Octavia continued, "I can experience a certain kind of fallback when I'm in those types of situations. And so, for me, it is really important to be able to keep commitments to myself around this. I know certain situations don't work out for me. I've done it multiple times, and I know better what's being served in some of those dynamics. And so I am very committed to not doing that. Even if it's somebody like Cornell, because I adore him. And in many ways, he's the love of my life. And I said, 'Even you. I will even leave you for myself.' Because that is what is required in this situation. I'm putting up boundaries with my mom now, too. I can't have the life sucked out of me by people, either intentionally or unintentionally. That is not how I want to be spending my life energy. I can do better by myself."

The Woman acts in integrity to the story that Octavia's written about the kind of relationship she wants, what she is willing to give to it, and her commitment to staying true to herself. Octavia explained, "The Woman feels more self-possessed, the part of me that can say this is not an effective strategy. So, I'm going to show up as my full self. The Woman allows me to bring my authentic self to my life and my relationships, even the vulnerabilities. It's the adult me. It's part of me showing up as a human."

The Sorceress

There were glimpses of another character, the *Sorceress*, in the scenes of Octavia's relationship with Cornell. Though it would be decades before the Sorceress came into her own, fully inhabiting the role she was cast to play, she had made fleeting appearances since Octavia was in her twenties. Even when the Sorceress was an ingenue, Octavia realized that she had a gift and ability to see people, to understand their perspectives and feel deeply into their experiences, even people who were much different than she. Octavia noted, "The Sorceress is the one who knows. I can see things and sense people's energies."

While Octavia was fascinated by this part of herself, she struggled to trust it, and struggled even more to allow her on the stage. She observed, "I've always had this fear of being too much. I'm always loving. But when I am in my Sorceress, I can be direct, piercing, and penetrating in my seeing of another. There's a quality that can just be a lot for people."

Octavia admitted, "There's a part of me that is embarrassed by the Sorceress, or feels embarrassed for other people. I protect people from her sometimes. I think that's who I'm protecting Cornell from. I think what Cornell loves and finds scary are the same things in different ways. The feedback that I've gotten from him is that I know him like nobody else knows him. And I see him, sometimes better than he sees himself. And who doesn't want that? Of course, we all want to be seen. *And* being seen is very penetrating, too. And one of Cornell's core wounds is shame, particularly about the parts of himself that he feels are ugly or unworthy, or parts that he's not proud of. And I see all of those things. And I challenge him around them in a way that I think other people don't or can't."

The Sorceress is direct, focused, intense. She's able to articulate the power struggles between partners even when she is one of them. She shows up in service to the relationship in order to reveal something to another. Octavia observed, "Some things just come out as these rants and power struggles between partners. And it's not to say I haven't gotten into those before. But as I've become more mature and honed more of my Sorceress and my Woman, I can articulate these things very clearly in a way that I think some of my partners find disarming."

The Sorceress challenged Cornell to grow through inquiry. And though Cornell was drawn to this part of Octavia, the Sorceress was often unable to be received by him. "The Sorceress is challenging for Cornell because he hasn't done his own work. He's conflict avoidant, which comes from his family upbringing. And he has a lot of shame and does a lot of hiding."

When the Sorceress is not welcome, Cornell withdraws, disappears, and it feels like a punishment to Octavia. She recalled, "Cornell would say, 'If I get mad, then I get mad. Just do it.' And I responded, 'And then you withdraw from me. You disappear.' I feel rejected and abandoned by him."

The Sorceress is a grace character, unifying, illuminating, integrating, in flow. But when others withdraw in reaction to the Sorceress, when she cannot be embraced and valued in her fullness, she falls back, relinquishing the stage to the Good Girl. Octavia noted, "There's just a lot of practice for the Good Girl. So it's not like I don't have any feelings when the Sorceress comes out. And I have to sometimes emotionally manage that afterwards on the back end."

The Good Girl tangles with the Sorceress. The powerful feminine energy that is the Sorceress comes on the scene to do what needs to be done. The Good Girl follows, feeling horrible, questioning herself. Sometimes Octavia feels remorse at having brought the Sorceress on stage, sometimes embarrassment. And other times, she holds the Sorceress in the wings because she fears that she will not be valued. The Good Girl takes the lead, going with the flow, not rocking the boat.

Octavia reflected, "There's a part of me that is afraid that this fierce feminine energy of the Sorceress is going to come out unbridled and burn some stuff down! I think it's the Good Girl who is afraid of that. What is my fear? Do I really feel like I'm going to hurt somebody? No, I feel like I'm going to do something to be rejected. Something that might be hard for somebody else, but that will get me rejected."

Indeed, the Good Girl comes out in protection, but not in protection of others. In protection of Octavia. Both characters were at play. And Octavia was navigating how to best cast them in the scenes of her life to serve the purpose of their roles without taking the whole set down.

Octavia felt the struggle of bringing the Sorceress forward consistently in the midst of all of the pulls within and outside of her to keep her under wraps. She challenged herself regularly to be more in her power, to not be embarrassed, to not hide. The ghosts of her full ensemble were prominent, and she worked ceaselessly to acknowledge their presence, to access their knowing, while not allowing them to ambush the scene.

Growing

The Sorceress not only stepped into the scenes of Octavia's personal life but had made fleeting guest appearances in her past professional roles. When the Sorceress came on stage in the scenes with Brenda, she missed her cues, always arriving late, and was somehow just out of Octavia's reach. Octavia caught glimpses of the Sorceress here and there in reflection on her fallback as she considered what she would have wanted to say or do in the moment, but the Sorceress wasn't on stage with her in the moment of action.

It was the Sorceress who Octavia wished had inquired to understand Brenda rather than to defend her competence. Octavia would have wanted to stand her ground internally, to hold onto her own perspective when she was challenged by Brenda. She just didn't have that capacity at that time. And the contextual gravitational pull created by a director with a hierarchical, power-over orientation did not lend itself to the Sorceress's presence on the scene.

But in Octavia's role at her new organization, the Sorceress was invited to serve in residency. Indeed, it was Octavia's wisdom that they sought when they hired her, that they coveted as she was promoted twice within two years, that was required of her in her leadership role in the organization.

Octavia saw her experience in her professional role and the way she showed up to it as a practice. She became intentional about developing the Sorceress, becoming more fluent, more nuanced, having more control over her and how and when she would come on the scene. Octavia wanted to cultivate the Sorceress to be more in her power, to not be embarrassed of her as the Good Girl so often was, to not look for an escape, as was the practice of the Unprotected Little. Over time and with intention, Octavia cultivated the Sorceress to serve as a costar alongside these other characters when her values and sense of self felt threatened, but also to take the lead.

Octavia's organization had a big mission—to foster the thriving of humankind. And there were ways in which the practices and structures within the organization's function were not aligned with its mission. Indeed, Octavia's organization fostered a much less complex context that trapped many in its gravitational pull. Octavia admitted, "I find myself having to watch that because that can show up in me, too. So I'm always asking, am I doing this because I know this is what is needed in this moment? Or am I being influenced by the organizational pull?"

Octavia admitted, "The fact is, I have multiple selves. And sometimes these different selves show up in fallback. So I'm constantly having to work to bring my fullest self, which includes a range of my capabilities, but especially the Sorceress and the Woman. Those other parts of me obviously are there, but they are not going to allow me to do the transformative work that I need to do because those are the ones that have shame." Octavia was not immune to the magnetism to a smaller space in her sense-making and acting. Her intentions, though, allowed her to hold steady.

Octavia was charged with shepherding transformational change and moving the organization and its structures into alignment with purpose. And this process entailed loss. As she undertook this work, she needed to hold the space for the dismay and the pain of the individuals who worked within it. She needed to connect to her intention, her purpose.

Octavia reflected, "It was very painful for the leadership in our organization to hear the ways employees thought they and the organization were not aligned with our stated mission. And it's not like I don't get triggered. I do have moments where I lose my shit with people, and I'm just like *enough*. But I cannot help this organization grow to its next level if I'm calcified. My practice was to remember I don't have to defend anything. Maybe this opinion that is being voiced is a good idea. Or maybe it's not a good idea. But I don't need to defend anything. And the minute I could just let go, I realized I don't have to hold onto anything. I can take it."

Octavia could hold her intention and her purpose if she could be like water, non-attached, able to move and flow in the midst of what felt like an attack. She was willing to stay in the muck of it, to examine it, to learn from it. Her intention became her North Star. She would ask herself, "How do I need to be in order to allow us to move?"

There is a marked difference between the way Octavia's characters performed their roles in the scene just described and the way those characters showed up in her interactions with Brenda three years prior. We might attribute this to casting and set, and certainly this played a role. The Sorceress and the Woman were invited into the play this time around. With Brenda, the Expert and the Unprotected Little commandeered the stage.

In truth, the full cast of Octavia's characters peppered both scenes. The difference was that Octavia had come to know them, had invited them into the glow of the ghost light and sat at their feet to learn their origins and their purpose. She was able to reclaim and work through experiences, threats, and aspects of her self born at an earlier time in her life. Now she was able to have the full ensemble there, each representing a part of herself. And she was able to cast them in the roles that would better meet her intentions.

Octavia identified another instance of growth in her interactions with the CEO of her organization. "I saw that he was entrenched in his views in the same way that Brenda was, and I wasn't going to change his mind. And I didn't need to change his mind. I needed to understand where he's coming from, to see where I might join him. I recognized that what I needed to do was not an advocacy, but an inquiry." Octavia's Expert was lingering at the edges of the stage, holding the cue cards that read "credibility...competence." Octavia could hold those as values, while not having the Expert run the scene. She realized there was a bigger intention and a different script that would help her meet it.

With Brenda, Octavia could see what was happening, could observe her self, but didn't have other abilities to bring. One, because she was in fallback. But two, because she hadn't yet fully developed these faculties that were cultivated through the Woman and the Sorceress. Octavia recalled, "I could see all of these things happening. But I couldn't do anything about it. I was caught. And I could see that I was caught, but I couldn't get out of it. And afterwards, I could see it, and take perspective, and even reflect on it with you, and go deeper. But I thought I would love to be able to shift in the moment. I know that you can't always do that because of whatever is coming up. But man, it would be nice to be able to do that at least a lot of the time, if not all the time."

"I feel like I have grown. Four years ago, I could do it sometimes, but not if I was really activated and triggered. Now, I'm much more capable of doing it in the moment." The Sorceress embodied the watching awareness and the capacity to respond from that place that Octavia had longed for in her interactions with Brenda.

While she had worked hard to cultivate the Woman and the Sorceress and to cue them onto the stage more prominently and without shame, and these characters were allowing her to grow in her capacities, she also found acceptance and appreciation for her full ensemble. Octavia observed, "I do want to hold more of my Sorceress and Woman energy. And these other characters, even though I might not prefer them all the time, maybe there's information when they show up to be welcomed. I'm trying to integrate them more, and not necessarily see them as problematic."

Indeed, there was value in each of these characters. Given the toxic relationships that had marked Octavia's past, the Unprotected Little's reflex to flee was wisdom. The Good Girl allowed others to feel her love, but also allowed Octavia to care for others, which she truly wanted to do. The Good Girl also protected Octavia from being rejected. The Woman acts in integrity to Octavia and expects mutuality. The Sorceress acts in service to purpose, revealing what needs to be seen. Each of these characters represented aspects of Octavia that were and still are integrally important to her. We might even call them superheroes. They just don't always perform in the ways that we expect our heroines to.

Octavia proclaimed, "We still get to be loved by the people in our lives even though we are imperfect. That's the complexity of it. We keep working at it. And we also accept ourselves as we are. I'm not always able to live into this, but I think part of my journey is not being on these constant self-improvement plans. I'm fine as I am now, even as I'm unfolding. And some of the being fine also includes some of my bullshit, too!"

"These characters don't have to be enemies or angels. I have these parts of myself. They show up under certain conditions. How do I recognize when they're showing up and then work with them in these different ways?"

Fallback is self-protective. It often looks and feels destructive. And to be sure, it can be. But when our fallback characters storm the stage of self, they are acting in protection of something we value, something that feels threatened. Rather than push them away, we would be wise to invite them in, to get to know them, to learn what it is they are there to teach us. Octavia had begun to embrace the full ensemble of her characters, to listen to them more. She began to cultivate the capacity to discern whether there was real risk in the scenes in which they were present or if there was just an old script leading to a conditioned response. She recognized that sometimes her fallback helps her to determine what the needed action is.

Over the years, we watched as these characters entered and exited the stage, blossomed and took the lead, and formed different relationships to each other. Ultimately, Octavia, having left the ghost light burning for them, would come to welcome each of them into her ensemble, embracing the lessons that they had come to teach her.

CHAPTER 16
YOUR TURN TO RECOVER AND GROW

You as the Director of the Scenes of Your Life

You have sat in this theater of self for some time now, venturing in at first tentatively with only a ghost light to illuminate the way. You have reflected upon your soliloquys and dialogues and ensemble performances. You have unearthed your origin stories and laid them bare, drawing from them the gifts that a truthful knowing of self can offer. You've discovered your values and your fears and have begun to know which characters are going to be cast by default in which scenes.

Now it is time to become the director of your own play, to connect to your intentions and allow those to illuminate the narrative that you wish to write. Perhaps you will find that you need to rewrite the script or at least rearrange the set. You may find that the story itself needs to shift. What worked for you before may seem like a peculiar story in a far-off land when you look at it through the lens of your current self and your current context. It's also important to recognize that the stories of who we are "supposed" to be may not be valid, possible, or even desirable at this time. Perhaps the screenplay needs to be adjusted. What better time than now to choose who we wish to be, to direct ourselves in the story of our lives that we are writing?

Exercise

Think about a future scene in the play of your life, one for which you may feel apprehension or concern that there's a high likelihood that you'll fall into the orchestra pit of fallback.

What is the setting? Who are the actors, the stakeholders, other than you?

What are your intentions for yourself in this scene?

What values do you fear may be threatened in this scene? What feels at risk as you think about walking on stage?

Which characters in your ensemble of self need to be on stage to best serve you in meeting your intentions while also protecting what you value?

Are there some nascent characters who also need to be cast?

What do they each contribute?

What role do they play?

What stage direction can you offer them? How will they dance together?

What set design needs to be put in place? What props, costumes, scaffolds will help set the stage for you to show up in alignment with your purpose – a quiet space for conversation, sneakers should you need to go for a walk, a good night's sleep, a grounding meditation?

What is the script you have running? Might you need to flip the script?

Put pen to paper and answer these questions.

Our hope is to anticipate when a scene might go awry. A dress rehearsal offers us the opportunity to review the script, determine which characters need to be on the stage and where, erect the set, have the necessary props at the ready, and make sure the costumes still fit. Perhaps most importantly, we determine if we need to flip the script.

Then… SHOWTIME. Step into the scene of your life knowing that you have rehearsed with thought and intention the way you wish to show up, the props you will need at the ready, the characters who will be cued onto the scene, and what purpose they each serve.

After the performance, write a review.

How did you do? Did the characters move together as you had hoped they would? Was their stage time well-balance? How were your characters received by the other actors in the scene? By the audience? How did it feel within you for your characters to dance together in this way? Are there other characters that need to be integrated? Does the scene need to be rewritten? The set rearranged?

Growth from fallback is supported by an everyday commitment to reflection, learning from and embracing mistakes, and trying to have a bigger mind. We can start to recognize the contexts in which our fallback is triggered. We will need to identify the set and scaffolds that are available to us in the scenes of our lives and acknowledge and plan ahead for the times when they may not be. We can connect to our intentions for how we show up on stage and what we wish the storyline to be. We can begin to be strategic about which of our characters should be cast in the scene and for what purpose. Rehearsing and acting and reviewing our performance offers the opportunity to experiment, to make course corrections, to expand our range of options.

CHAPTER 17
EPILOGUE

Diego

Over the course of the two months following "the breaking," through letters, negotiations, and time, the urgency of the decision—Ellie or Kyra—dissipated. Ellie backed off of her demands for Diego to choose, thereby creating the space for Diego to be with Kyra without immediate imperatives to wind their relationship down and without walking away from his marriage. The Wolverine and the Shamed Quitter were cued to exit stage left. Diego could maintain some illusion of P3, at least externally. And the Cautious Ditherer was authorized to lope around the expanse of the stage.

I would accompany Diego for the next six years. During that time, Diego would befriend the shadowy characters that had burst upon the stage in his fallback with Kyra, that had in fact been in the scenes of his life for years, even though he had not heretofore shined the spotlight on them. He would come to know the values they were there in protection of. He would watch them dance together on the stage of his life, at first without choreography and then, over time, with him more frequently orchestrating their steps. And he would invite new characters into his cast and into the dance of his development.

EPILOGUE

Diego experimented with casting his characters in a way that served him, that served the intention of the scene. Instead of the ping-ponging that had marked his rapid transformation between Diego, the good guy, and Diego, the villain, he was able to enact more of a smooth shuttling. He could see this playing out with the Wolverine in his interactions with Ellie.

"I was able to move between the part of me that defends boundaries clearly, that wants to be clear about what it means for me to win and what it means for me to be safe and in control, and the part of me that can project love and kindness and generosity. And over time I could bring both of those almost in the same sentence, in the same moment, as opposed to snapping."

His falling back, rather than representing a decline in his sense-making, became part of the mechanism that allowed Diego to spring forward, to navigate the spectrum of his development more smoothly. He more frequently was able to not push away those earlier aspects of self, but instead to utilize their tools.

Diego was increasingly able to see the gifts that his fallback characters offered, sometimes alongside the loss. In Diego's personal relationship, the presence of the Cautious Ditherer had mixed implications. Five years after "the breaking," Diego observed, "I had not realized how, when there is a separation, when there is a conflict, and it wedges into a relationship, that unless there is a very deliberate effort to heal, time just corrodes and widens the rift. And that's what's happening between me and Ellie. I don't think I've ever had the single-minded intent of healing the relationship. I wanted to keep my options open. And that has widened the gap to a point where it's not any longer a livable relationship. And I don't know that I regret that necessarily. Because letting it play out this way has its own light."

The ambivalence of the Cautious Ditherer led to the further disintegration of his marriage to Ellie. Yet, over time, Diego realized it also enabled the strengthening of his relationship with his children. Diego noted, "Had I forced a divorce five or six years ago, my relationship with the kids would have been shaken quite a bit. And because things have lasted so long, they have had to come in the open for conversations as a family, conversations one-on-one with the kids. And today if we were to divorce, my relationships with the kids are stronger than they ever were."

Indeed, the lingering of the Cautious Ditherer on the stage of his life in the years following "the breaking" with Kyra made space for a new character, the *Independent Father*, to be cast. Diego explained, "The Independent Father came from the terror that I had at one point of losing my relationship with the kids along with my marriage. That's a very clear threat that Ellie bandies around all the time. And for the longest time, I took it as absolutely true. I was subject to the idea."

But as the Cautious Ditherer dithered, a new possibility emerged. "I forced myself to imagine a world in which I could have divorced from Ellie and yet had a meaningful relationship with the kids. So, the Independent Father was born out of necessity. And it was born out of insight that those equals I was holding were not true."

"If the Cautious Ditherer hadn't been on the scene in 2015, I would have broken my marriage, I would have married Kyra, and I don't know where my relationship with the kids would be today. Having time play a role here has allowed me to preserve what is the most important part of what this relationship with Ellie has created, which is our kids. Had I showed up as I was capable six years ago, being cerebral and trying to convince people that what I'm doing is right, it was not going to cut it. By being vulnerable, by accepting their perspective, that has changed the conditions quite a bit."

As we reflect on our fallback characters and the roles they play in the scenes of our lives, we often realize that they offered a gift, often intentionally, sometimes just by happenstance, that perhaps we were not able to see and appreciate at the time.

"The Cautious Ditherer unwittingly created the time for the Independent Father to develop. But the Cautious Ditherer is not the one who was having those vulnerable conversations with the kids. That was the Independent Father in concert with the Powerful Holder," Diego observed.

The *Powerful Holder* holds all perspectives, allows more voices in the conversation, allows a more equal balance of power. The Powerful Holder had been present in the scenes of Diego's relationship with Kyra as they imagined what a future together could be even before the fallback episode. But Diego struggled to cast him consistently in the scenes of his life with his family. Over the years, Diego honed his directorial capacity, not only with his children, but also with Ellie.

Diego recalled, "In the past, my conversations with Ellie around what to do with our couple were jagged, were sort of a sequence of exerting pressure, yielding, exerting pressure, yielding, pleading. And that was not working in any way. We could not get to common ground. We could only get to *I get my way this time; you might get your way next time*, through a process of power and force."

Diego continued, "I realized that we were not going to get any agreement unless I was capable of holding her wants, my wants, clearly; her pain, my pain, clearly. And then not excluding any of that, but being able to process whatever decisions, actions, we needed to take in the context of all of this. So, the Powerful Holder has been the main character on stage to get us to the agreement. And Ellie's never felt as good about an agreement. All of the past agreements we made, all of those felt imposed by me in a way. This is probably the time when the balance of power has been least unequal. There have been more voices in the process—the therapists, the kids—and I have been really mindful, paying attention not to act out of just power."

The agreement that Ellie and Diego came to was to begin the process of divorce. The decision, at last, was made. The Cautious Ditherer moved quietly into the wings, making way for a new character to step onstage—the *Co-Creator*.

In the past, when faced with complex problems for which there was no easy answer, Diego cast the Cautious Ditherer. The Cautious Ditherer was in Diego's head creating spreadsheets of pros and cons. This casting of the Cautious Ditherer when the most confounding decisions were up always led to failure because the Cautious Ditherer could only see the loss in each decision and was unable to choose.

But the Co-Creator is not driven to decision by emotion but by trust in life, in the system, understanding that the body, not the mind or emotions, knows. Diego explained, "The Co-Creator is the part of me that does not take personal agency as being absolute, that doesn't believe that one can shape everything to one's will. He appreciates the fact that things are constantly changing, and we can never predict where they will go, and that any decision that looks good in certain circumstances will look very different under different circumstances. And so trying to force a decision, trying to use my personal agency to create the conditions that I want, is not necessarily wise—definitely not wise in situations that are complex and moving fast enough. The perspective of the Co-Creator is to let the world do the work for you. Let the fruit fall off the tree, as opposed to go and snatch it."

When the Co-Creator came on the scene, there seemed to be less turmoil and angst. There was a trust in a greater knowing beyond self. Diego began to recognize that he cannot force the path of things—particularly complex things—with good result.

Diego observed, "I'm trying not to rush to conclusions or to solutions. I'm trying just to notice what's happening, what's becoming possible, not possible, what makes me happy. And I know that there will be a change, but I have no sense of the contours of that change. I'm avoiding rushing to a solution."

Yet, the Co-Creator is not yet fully integrated. Diego caught himself in recognition of this. He observed, "It's interesting, the language of 'avoiding rushing to a solution' indicates how there's the tug of war with my own self, right?" Diego still must "avoid." It does not yet happen naturally.

Diego had become more comfortable in his directorial role. He had come to realize that the characters comprising his ensemble would not arrive on stage polished, having remembered their lines precisely, already familiar with the cues. He would need to develop them, all of them, to allow them to hone their skill in performing their role in the action. There would inevitably be missteps. And that was okay.

In the years following his fallback with Kyra, having begun to make the connections and become aware of patterns, Diego began to notice his fallback more quickly and even to cultivate the capacity to respond differently. Diego observed, "I notice myself, and I am more self-reliant in my ability to pull myself out of the ditch. Having conceptualized the experience of getting out of the pit, I've created the scaffold in my mind that I can summon when I need it. My fallback still happens every bit as often. Parts of me that get triggered are still here. They haven't disappeared. But the other parts of me come to the rescue much, much faster."

Robbin

After seven weeks of losing ground, a shrinking context, and a contracting self that had marked Robbin's spring of 2020, summer at last arrived. And with it came the return of Charles's and Elsa's nanny. The nanny's arrival ushered in a lightening of the heaviness, of the grip that had constrained Robbin's sense-making and acting during the first two months of the pandemic and the shame that had been companion to how he frequently showed up with his family. As the necessity to serve every need for his family in every moment lessened, Robbin began to see glimpses of his former self. He began to pull the disparate parts of himself back into some kind of whole—rag-tag, duct-taped, and disheveled as it had become.

Robbin declared, "I'm out! Just like that, I'm out of fallback!" And for a time, he was.

Then came fall, and the start of school for Charles. And while a return to school would any other year promise more adult freedom, 2020 was a year like no other. Charles would begin his education at home with Robbin as his instructional aide. Absent the structures that would allow Robbin to succeed, to step up, to propel he and his family to security, and himself to the existence beyond his four walls that he so longed for, the contextual gravitational pull of his surround dragged Robbin into the valley of his sense-making, marked by hopelessness and despair. The Drowning lurched onto the stage.

"I feel like I'm in a holding pattern of *ready, set, stop,*" Robbin shared. "I think there's a key difference in that I could let myself off the hook in the spring, because that was a fucking surprise. And there's a layer of *should have seen this coming* with regard to the fall, because it's less surprising that I would have to step back, that I would have to retreat, that I hadn't planned."

Robbin was coming to recognize the scenes of his life, the settings that beckoned some of his shadowy characters on the stage. And he realized that there weren't going to be many set changes these days. He better figure out how to work the equipment.

"When I am out of fallback, I feel relief that I'm not in the throes of it. But also, I need to acknowledge that the circumstances that gave rise to it are probably just beginning. This is not blowing over. It's just life now and will be with some serious edits to assumptions that we had about how life worked for some time to come." Robbin noted, "If we're thinking of it as a room in the house, it sucked to feel locked in there, not knowing where the light switch was, knowing that there were other rooms. But I think my relationship to it now is, you need to learn how to inhabit this room. Because we're going back."

Robbin mused, "I guess the real trick is to let those moments wound as deeply as they need to, to recognize what they can tell us."

Over the coming months, Robbin would familiarize himself with the rooms that represented earlier parts of himself. He would come to know their layout, sit in their hardbacked chairs, rifle through the drawers. He would spend minutes at a time gazing into the mirror hanging on the wall, watching as it reflected back to him someone far different from the person he remembered himself being. He sat in these rooms of his smaller self with a desire to get to know them, to understand what he had not paid close enough attention to during his original inhabitation.

Robbin reflected, "So much of my own maturation process has relied on banishing. And there are violent consequences to that. Right now, my coherent story for my life is getting blown up. And I'm having to reevaluate all of these transitions and recognize that while I'm accustomed to thinking of myself as the hero, I've been kind of a nitwit in a lot of them. And it's okay to not think of yourself as the hero who did right anymore. But one of the things that's striking to me is that I had believed that in order to move out of the pain of the earlier, less-complex phases of my life, I needed to grow up and be something else. Banish him. Set him aside. But it all seems too extreme. And I'm beginning to wonder if there is some kind of reconfiguration I can do where I'm not sentenced to a lifetime of some pattern."

"Because part of me wishes I'd done a lot of these things differently. And another part of me wonders *from where you were, was that even possible?* Perhaps this is what growth is, this messy process. And if you want those pieces back, you have to go get them when you're capable of handling them. Because there's no way to have the wherewithal to do this cleanly at any given stage."

Development for Robbin, as is the case for so many of us, had heretofore necessitated rejecting that which came before so something new could come. In its extreme form, it may be a complete banishment or destruction of that part of self in order to perpetuate the stories we tell ourselves about who we are, who we've been. Now, he was beginning to realize that instead of a pushing away, a deconstruction of who he had fashioned himself to be was the path to growth. A fracturing of the constructed self was necessary in order for integration to occur.

"I think that on the personality level, there's always a breaking of something going on in order to integrate. Integration is not a smooth, clean process. It involves dismantling something that was there before. And I imagine that there may be ways in which I can lean into the dismantling process, rather than having it happen to me."

Over the coming six months, Robbin would experiment with leaning into the deconstruction, not so he could reject those parts of self, but so that he could bring them back in, to tune in to what they were trying to tell him.

Robbin reflected, "More and more these fallback episodes are feeling like prompts to integration. After these involuntary jerks—and they were violent jerks—I'm realizing Mr. Fuck You with all of his positive qualities, too, needs to be let back into the house, or out of the basement, or wherever he's been confined. Bring him in. Make him part of the family. I feel a curiosity to welcome in parts of myself that I would have shunned because of the expectation that I show up as my highest or most evolved self all of the time. Self-Sovereign me will bring things to the table, will bring *me* to the table, and participate in ways that a Socialized or a Self-Authoring me decidedly will not.[1] And some of those ways are perfectly delightful."

Robbin started to rearrange the furniture in those rooms of his smaller self, to make it more comfortable for his needs now. He took down the 90s hair metal band posters and neatly stored them in a drawer. All but one. The picture of Robbin Crosby from the band Ratt still hung, an homage to who he had been then, a part of self that remained now. He picked up the guitar he hadn't held since college, plugged it into the amp, and began to play the music from his first foray in this room. It melded into a melody with the music from his present.

Robbin mused, "I've watched as Charles has just been spellbound as he's seen me play, and Elsa dances to it. And it's like, wow! There's something that I get to bring to my family that feels like a very personal and rich part of me, that adds a missing ingredient that wasn't here. It feels like a welcoming back of a banished character."

The *Dream Warrior*, the character that Robbin was welcoming back, causes all sorts of mischief when the ghost light is out. And then Robbin turns on the light, and the Dream Warrior takes the stage with his amp and his lovely equipment and regales the audience of his children with his performance. Robbin remarked, "It's a reminder that there's real power in this part of me and power for good. Harness that, and the kids are enchanted." Robbin had flipped the script.

"So I think the question is, *How do I act the part of conductor?* It's a spirit of curiosity and welcoming. *How can we be here together? What can we do here together?* I feel like this isn't about managing those parts of myself as though some of them were disruptive. But it's really about realizing that they all have unique and individual value that can only be expressed if they're all playing their instruments in the orchestra and have room to do that. Fallback has brought me face-to-face with the full ensemble."

Robbin had come to see the value in integrating the full orchestra of self, big and small. He realized that, just as the younger parts of self didn't need to be pushed away, they also didn't need to take center stage or show up as a solo act as they often had in the past. In fact, Robbin thought his ensemble could benefit from a casting call for new players, to harmonize with the old.

"I have been imagining the best-case scenario as me as someone in charge of a Milanga dance party, an Argentine tango dance party. In Argentine tango, when you're dancing with your partner, you're listening with your entire physicality. And the *Milanga Master* as I envision it is setting the stage for lots of people to do that, creating the soft connective tissue."

Robbin had also begun to think about how he might develop his existing characters. The Turf Roarer was beginning to find expression through the Dream Warrior. Robbin envisioned a new character, the *Game Warden*, as the communicator of expectations. The Milanga Master would be the heralder of aspirations, setting the stage for the full ensemble to dance together. These new characters were meant to complement the existing ensemble, not paint them into the background.

Robbin reflected back on the stories that he'd shared, on the experiences he'd had, on the cast that had shown up on the stage of his life over the course of the year that we were in exploration together. He could see now all of the times when the full ensemble of his characters was on stage and also in the wings, perhaps pulling the strings because they weren't invited into the spotlight. When he turned on the ghost light within self, something shifted.

He noted, "I've had throughout my life this tendency to look at who I was a few months ago and kind of cringe. And I'm not having that at all right now. I've turned some kind of corner where I can look at who I've been in the last year with great appreciation and not feel a need to spin him in any way, not feel a need to make apologies for him or have it be slightly different. I receive these quotes you share with me with pride. I appreciate the congruence of myself over the last year, and I like who I'm hearing."

When we embrace fallback, we find humility, gratitude, and acceptance of the full, rich suite of humanity that is us. True, honest, earnest, solid, stable, sustainable growth can only happen when we accept once and for all that it is all of us. In integrating the full ensemble of characters that make us up, we come to appreciate the congruence in our incongruence.

Octavia

As Octavia's Sorceress was explicitly cast in the play of her professional life, she was able to intentionally cultivate the Sorceress's capacities, to learn and grow from her, to not feel embarrassed by her as she once had. The Sorceress was present as Octavia held the space for transformation of herself and others, and of organization. The Sorceress had the capacity to notice in the moment, to engage in action inquiry[2] in real time.

Octavia could see glimpses of the Good Girl and even the Expert, but they were merely glimpses. Octavia befriended these characters, understood them, and welcomed them into her ensemble. Because her characters were now welcomed into the theater of self, they didn't need to cause such a ruckus to be seen. They were not stealing the show. They were open to different casting configurations and script changes that allowed Octavia to be more aligned with her intentions.

As the Sorceress gained more stage time, and Octavia became more comfortable in this role, she began to welcome the Sorceress into the scenes of her personal life, in her relationship with Cornell. She desired to be fully herself with him, to stay close to her experience and theirs, as it is. She wished to share her experience, needs, desires, tensions, joys, and disappointments with him without contempt or demand. She longed to trust the process and unfolding of their relationship and both she and Cornell in it.

Octavia shared, "I have been in a deep relational practice with my beloved that involves me holding both of us in regard and honoring our sovereignty of experience, need, and desire. This has involved a series of hard and beautiful conversations and movement. It's been beautiful to witness, even in its difficulty. It's the type of relational space that I've longed for for years. It does not look the way I envisioned it, or rather, it's not necessarily eliciting the outcome that I expected."

"As a result of this ongoing relational practice, we decided to move into another expression of our relationship beyond the romantic, monogamous commitment that we were previously in. We still love each other, but we don't know what our next movements will look like. We are stepping into the unknown relational space together grounded in our love for and commitment to each other. It feels right, and I am heartbroken."

"As I sat in the open space of this decision and movement, I cried and became very quiet for stretches of time. Old friends and demons came to visit, and I sat with all of my knowing and unknowing. Feelings of being utterly alone. Feelings of being unwanted and unloved. Feelings of not belonging. Feeling unprotected or not taken care of. Neediness and unmet needs. Also feelings of being loved, of possibility and spaciousness, fear, gratitude, resignation, heartbreak. I sat in these with all sorts of storylines just beneath the surface, and also with no storyline. I sat in the ground of my being with another without need or desire to reframe or run away or blame anyone."

Octavia reflected, "That's the Sorceress energy. In the moment, being able to be fully in the surprise or the heartbreak or the whatever of my experience. I had a lot of feelings come up. There were moments where I might get activated and upset and some other character might show up. But I could hang in there, and then move out of that moment and to another possibility. But I didn't have to act out. I could take the best timely action in that moment. Which with him was occasionally sharing some of what was showing up for me. And that might be all I need to do ever, with anybody. This would not have been available to me five years ago. I do have more capacity now to work in these ways."

As Octavia engaged in the series of conversations with Cornell that resulted in the dissolution of their romantic relationship, she was intentional about which characters needed to come on the scene, when they were cued, what they offered. The Sorceress, the character that she had been explicitly cultivating for years, the one she knew she needed as part of her ensemble, played the lead. Yet hers was not a solo act. Octavia's full ensemble was on the stage, allowing her to pay attention to her fears, to be true to her values, to hold herself in integrity, while also honoring and caring for the needs and integrity of Cornell.

The Sorceress is wise and knowing and has the ability to penetrate others' experience. She can hold space that allows transformation to happen. But without the other characters in Octavia's ensemble there to remind her of her need to feel safe and protected, her desire to care for others, her wish to be in integrity to herself, the Sorceress, even in all of her power and glory, can be hollow and detached. The Sorceress is built from and upon the whole messy human that is Octavia. She is possible because of the rich ensemble of which she is a part. And Octavia had begun to enlist the full cast in the important roles they served in the play of her life.

CHAPTER 18
LEAVING THE GHOST LIGHT BURNING FOR OTHERS

I began research for this book in 2015. Having situated the phenomenon of fallback within the broader theory of adult development, I wanted to understand what it looked like, what it felt like, how it presented, how individuals made sense of it through their own lived experience. I never intended for this to be a longitudinal study. But life and insecurities and pandemics happen. And in the intervening timeframe, I had the honor of accompanying three individuals on their journeys along the meandering pathways of coming to know themselves, their ensemble of characters, and the world they live in anew.

Indeed, we were all coming to know the world anew and with increasing ferocity and intimacy as we faced up close what had seemed for many of us during our brief lifetimes, with our limited historical memories, to be vague and distant threats. Many of us, myself included, had a short view on reality. We weren't paying enough attention to the long game, or the way that the long game had penetrated daily life so insidiously that we hardly even noticed that things had changed, or in some cases, that they had not.

Increasingly over the course of the last seven years, life as we knew it changed, and we couldn't help but be changed by it. Those things we had turned a blind eye to before were knocking at our door. In many cases, there was no knock before the door crashed in upon us. And so many of us found an earlier shadowy and dark version of ourselves in the person who rose from the debris as we were assaulted by the unrelenting uncertainty, fear, anxiety, volatility, and threat that permeated every corner of our lives and crept into the corners of our developmental house.

The past two years alone have forced an undeniable and inescapable comeuppance. Humankind has been made to confront and reckon with the many ways we do not live in alignment with our intentions and values and the effect that disconnect has had on the species as a whole and on subgroups of the species that we implicitly assumed were less deserving.

The circumstances and conditions and threats of the past seven years since I began researching this book have brought into sharp focus the prevalence of fallback within each of us individually. They have also shined a spotlight on the broader implications for a system, a culture, a society trapped in earlier sense-making under the weight of living through these unprecedented times.

So when Jennifer Garvey Berger, Bill Torbert, David McCallum, Chuck Palus, Susanne Cook-Greuter, Bob Kegan, and I convened on a spring day in 2021, the implications of the relationship we form to our fallback, not only for our individual illumination but also for the illumination of others, seemed incredibly relevant.[1] As we witnessed the decline in our communities, societies, and the world at large, we couldn't help but wonder what role fallback may play at the collective and systemic levels—what the implications were and what the possibilities may be.

Berger described collective fallback as "the notion that the context we're in actually creates the conditions for us to be, to come into, a smaller version of ourselves." Berger explained, "I think the political discourse in the United States, for example, creates the conditions for people to by and large not be able to engage in useful, thoughtful conversation—even those people who can do useful, thoughtful conversation with one another in other contexts. I wonder about the ways our collective isolation contributes to our inability to take perspectives, or to reach into compassion, or to recognize ourselves.

I wonder about how the fact that we don't bump into each other reduces our perspective-taking capacity and also reduces our access to feedback that would illuminate some of these smaller selves. And then there's just the nervous system. How much are we actually living in the sympathetic nervous system and unable to break through to the parasympathetic nervous system, which is where I think we make many of these choices that are more developmentally sophisticated?"

Context matters significantly in how we are able to show up to our lives and the challenges we face. The context that we are living in, permeated as it has been in recent history by ever-increasing existential threat, invites the smaller selves of each of us as individuals, and in so doing beckons the smaller self of the collective. We see our individual patterns—a retreat to earlier parts of self and less complex sense-making—reflected in the collective. We see the collective patterns oriented toward a fight-flight-freeze response reflected in individuals.

Palus noted, "Susanne Cook-Greuter has said that fallback, at least one kind of it, is when everything falls down, the whole structure falls apart. So it's not just a temporary readjustment. There's a collapse of the feeling of any ability to get out of it. It does feel like that's something that's happening right now." Palus explained, "In American history we've shared some ideal of transcendence. The American story of overcoming, and transforming, and becoming interdependent with one another, I think that's always been a guiding light. And I think we've lost that somehow. There are these fantasies that not only are we not collectively progressing, but collectively there's something evil going on that has to be overthrown."

"I wonder about whether some of these things needed to tip over into some place, get composted back into the soil, and then grow back into the ideal in some new way," observed Berger. "One of the things that the theorist Spring Cheng talks about is that developmental theory as we have it is only a piece of a cycle. We only talk about growth.[2] And the other thing that happens in a natural cycle is decline, and specifically composting. And this idea of what is fallback composting? I've been very intrigued by this notion of what happens in decline, in the fallow space."

We might define fallback composting as the natural process of recycling the matter in our sense-making in a way that allows the valuable fertilizer of our earlier selves to enrich the developmental soil of the self that is growing. Indeed, fallback composting is exactly the process that has been described throughout this book. Berger wondered how the decline and sometimes the death that fallback calls us to may not only be pivotal for our growth as individuals, but also integral to our growth as a collective.

"I feel that the social implications for our conversation are really critical," remarked McCallum. "We don't need developmental theory to let us know that entrenched, generational poverty, for instance, creates very powerful cycles of this kind of fallback behavior. And yet, it's amazing how individuals can grow through that kind of experience if they have one or two people creating the holding environment, to believe in them, and to help them move forward. I think about the moral obligations we have, knowing what we know, in terms of offering reinforced rationale and logic for dealing with really critical issues where people are facing these extreme circumstances. And a lot of it must be addressed at a much deeper level. At a spiritual, psychological level, we need to do some inner work as a people, as collectives and communities of peoples."

Berger remarked, "I wonder about the spirituality aspect as a form of coaxing the composting, making this fertile. Because you can just have piles of crap that don't compost and contribute to soil. Or you can have this thing that actually is part of a healthy ecosystem as it returns nutrients back into our base in some way."

McCallum reflected, "Chuck mentioned the way in which, at least in this U.S. context, we've veered in not just an individual direction, but in an individualistic direction, which has become toxic and lost the sense of a greater common good. I think this particular phase within our country actually requires us to move in a communitarian direction. Not the camps and tribes direction, but one that can tolerate the ambiguity of our differences and maintain empathy."

McCallum continued, "I think about the power of small communities that are diverse that can ask questions of one another and explore and create the safe spaces that make it safer also to enter into the bigger spaces. It may seem like a small thing, but for those of us who have relatively diverse circles where we're interacting, this is just one of so many dimensions that I think help to address the complexity that we're facing at a larger level, and where we draw support. I think this is an interesting time for folks to convene those kinds of groups, and the willingness to bring in the polarities, politically and racially and sexually. Because climate change, the refugee displacement that's going to happen, all of these things require us to rise to a new level of both vulnerability and courage."

McCallum noted the importance of articulating the steps, mapping out the process and the muck we are going to have to trudge through in order to cultivate the parts of self that will help us better align with purpose as we face into the changing world.

As McCallum offered ideas for how we may collectively engage the gaps that societies are facing and the role that our collective fallback plays in these, I couldn't help but think of Octavia's orientation toward transforming self in order to transform her organization, in order to contribute to the flourishing of humankind. Octavia observed, "If you are talking about personal-to-societal transformation, you cannot transform societies without transforming yourself, because you are a fractal of that society. And as leaders, if we pretend we are outside this paradigm, we can't be part of the transformation happening."

Octavia also knew that we can't do it to others. We must do it with them. We must be open to change within as we are also changing what is outside of us. Octavia could see what was happening within her, happening within others, happening within the organization, happening within society. These are all connected, all part of the system, with each part also shifting the system. And as David suggested, our smaller communities, the places where we live and work, may be where we need to start.

Creating the Conditions for the Illumination of Others

Berger observed, "As a leadership characteristic, having a relationship to our own fallback that is developmental, supportive, and helpful would be extraordinary because it would be about experimentation, about forgiveness, about seeing new sets of possibilities where you're not presented with new sets of possibilities."

In fact, Berger had been thinking about what leaders would need to put in place in order to invite people to access the fullness of themselves in all their messy complexity at least since we began exploring the fallback phenomenon together nearly a decade ago.

At the time, she suggested that leaders need to first create a context and culture that enables individuals to bring their bigger selves. And second, to create a space that allows individuals not to—to make the space of fallback a safe space, too.[3]

Context matters greatly in creating both the conditions that prompt fallback and also the conditions for acceptance, recovery, and growth. This knowledge is powerful not only in the shepherding of one's own development but also the fostering of development in others—in groups, in organizations, and in communities—in that it emphasizes the importance of context to the developmental capacity we and others are able to bring. When our contexts invite us to bring our bigger selves, when the conditions exist for our most complex selves to be present, when we are authorized and appreciated for that aspect of our being, we show up accordingly.

Berger suggested that in groups, fallback can be talked about. Teams can identify the pulls on smallness in their individual members, identify pulls on bigness, and build psychologically spacious environments that pull people toward their bigger selves. Environments supporting this include dynamic states that are safe and empowering and that allow and prompt deeper insight, perspective, and safe reflection without judgment or threat.[4]

We can see clearly the role that context played in Octavia's ability to bring the characters who were most aligned with her intentions into the scenes of her organizational life. In the hierarchical, dismissive environment that Brenda created, Octavia's bigger self was not welcome. It was the characters of her smaller self that were cued onto the scene—the Expert to defend her credibility, the Unprotected Little in protection of her safety. Not that those characters were welcomed by Brenda, either. They were just the only parts of self that Octavia could fit onto the constricting stage of that environment. Only after the fact, outside of the circumstances, could Octavia even begin to conjure the Woman and the Sorceress.

Yet the context of Octavia's new organization was much different. Octavia noted, "I feel like the Sorceress is welcomed at my job. I was put in this role because of the Sorceress, and my boss said that to me explicitly, 'I want you in this role because of your wisdom.'" There is something about being invited, not in spite of but precisely because this is what you bring. This beautiful invitation-turned-authorization allowed the Sorceress, the part of self that allows Octavia to be in alignment with her intentions and purpose, to claim the stage.

Octavia was able to bring her bigger self to her role because she felt seen, heard, and respected. Her personhood was not at risk. She felt held, not trapped, so she didn't have to locate the nearest escape hatch. And she could begin to cultivate the characters within self that allowed her to create a welcoming context for others in their fullness.

While Octavia's organizational context invited her to bring her biggest self because that's where they wanted to get to, it also occupied an earlier developmental space, a space that Octavia has within her, too. The conditions of the organization, driven by their mission for societal and individual transformation, welcomed the Sorceress. Yet the conditions of the earlier developmental context, marked by less complexity, going along to get along, and stasis were also present. While the Sorceress was often center stage in Octavia's role, there were other characters in Octavia's ensemble who were present, too, cued by the gravitational pull to a less complex space within the organization. And that was okay.

Octavia had come to recognize the full cast of characters that make up her ensemble. She knew that she often had the capacity to bring the Sorceress on the stage, particularly because the context invited her to do so. Yet her other characters were still lingering in the wings, prepared to bound on the stage if something she valued felt at risk. That Octavia could see that it was safe to bring the earlier parts of her, even while the context explicitly invited her more complex self to be present, was a gift.

In order to invite others into the work, we need to normalize fallback. To do this, we must name it. Name that we, every one of us, are not consistent in the way we show up from day-to-day, moment-to-moment, task-to-task. Name that there are moments when the full array of our developmental capacities are on display, at the ready. And there are many moments when they are closed behind the doors of our developmental house, and we are just...well...smaller.

When we deny the suffering of self, the anguish and despair, the smallness and shadows, we leave no space for others to bring their own. We set an expectation for some kind of superhuman steeling against the forces of our time that are so vehemently assaulting the world as we know it and the self that we know. Just because we don't name it, doesn't mean it doesn't exist. Within us. In the space between us. The unspoken doesn't go away. It just festers in its abandonment.

When we claim our own fallback, when we reveal our full selves to others, when we tap into the whole of our humanity, we create a space safe for others to claim, reveal, and tap into theirs. And that's something we can work with. But first, we need to illuminate the darker corners within ourselves.

Octavia desired to bring her full self, to own and embrace it in the spotlight for others to see, so that they may also shine the light on their own messy complexity. There was a humility about the way she brought herself to her work. A sense of, *I understand where you are now. I've got that in me, too.* One of the gifts of coming into relationship with our fallback is that it allows us to be of use to others and to have compassion in seeing these smaller parts of them that also exist in us.

Octavia held the container for others to show up in their fullness. She did so from a space of compassion, seeing herself in the struggle as she witnessed the struggle in others. And allowing it to be. The entirety of it, light and shadow.

Recovery from fallback is often characterized by awareness and vulnerability not only to self but also to others. Surrounding ourselves with people who are willing to point out our fallback, to offer honest, direct, timely, feedback, can aid in our ability to take perspective on ourselves in our smallness. Our connections with others serve as anchors in the construction of self.

McCallum remarked, "I have found a lot of benefit in discovering my blind spots through not only the fallback experience, but then the feedback I get about the fallback, and working with it, and discovering things I wasn't seeing. Somebody who's very important to me said, 'At times, I'm used to you giving thimblefuls of attention because you're doing too many things.' And I thought to myself, *What?! Oh my gosh! This is how I'm being experienced by someone?* And then I decided to check. Oh, there are several people who experience this thimblefuls-of-attention because of my multitasking or my work addictions."

Our willingness to hold others while also holding them accountable through their experience of fallback plays a pivotal role in their ability to reflect upon and accept their full selves. This is true both in personal relationships and in leadership roles. When we understand that development is not always onward and upward, that we as humans are indeed the full catastrophe, we have greater empathy for others and how they make sense of the world. And this acceptance, of self and by others, may just be what allows us to recover and grow.

While fallback may serve as a catalyst for springing forward, it doesn't always. Importantly, development necessitates the explicit intent of those who participate to grow.

Octavia realized that in order to create the context for others to bring their bigger selves, she needed to invite them without attachment to whether they accepted her invitation. Octavia noted, "I'm very clear, it is a choice. I have to constantly remind myself, this organization can grow or not grow. That is not my responsibility. My responsibility is to create the conditions for growth and to create the invitation. I can reveal you to yourself because I have that capacity. And I can show up with presence and accompany you. But I am not responsible for your growth or this community's growth. And if you choose not to grow, that's fine. I'm not going to judge you for it."

Octavia knew that to take up her role, to exercise leadership, she would have to be willing to disappoint people when she gave the work back to them to do, when they were looking to her to solve the problems on their behalf. But in fallback, as in leadership, our job is not to do the work for others, but to invite them into the work.

Fallback Composting in the Collective

What we know about how to illuminate fallback in self and how to create the space for fallback to be illuminated in others may offer us clues about the nutrients needed in order to compost our collective fallback. A holding environment that welcomes the fullness of self. The opening up of safe spaces to begin the forthright conversations about what invites our bigger selves on the scene, and also to welcome the smaller parts. The capacity to see and name the smaller parts in self, which engenders compassion for the smaller parts of others. The willingness to see and be seen fully and authentically by another.

Transforming self while transforming society means that we have to open ourselves up to the gains and the losses that come with deeply exploring our assumptions and ways of being, our history and our desired future. Just as we as individuals must mind the gap between our espoused values and the way we are actually showing up, unpack the origin stories that have brought us to this place, and explore how we might seek to live more in line with our intentions, so must we as a collective.

We need to also acknowledge that this purposeful exploration of the place of decline so that something better may grow will entail pain. As we work the nutrients into the soil, our personal and societal traumas will be uncovered, will be poked and prodded, as the tending reveals the harms we, our organizations, and our societies have done. The paradox of fallback may be that pain and suffering are necessary for growth to occur.

When we think about development and growth, we often think of all of the upsides, the benefits, the gains. We need to recognize that as we come to know ourselves and the world anew, there is a dying of the self and the world we have known. What we rarely acknowledge but is nonetheless true is that there is loss and pain in growth, in development.

In fallback, too, there is loss. There is decline. There is suffering. There is something that we must experience as absent that *can* snap us back to attention, make us notice, make us question. And this noticing might bring us closer to the divine within us.

Sophie Sabbage wrote, "There are some battles that can only be fought on your knees. Usually when you come face-to-face with your own powerlessness, and the only moves you have left are to bow your head in reverence and to clasp your hands in prayer."[5] Indeed, I believe that the inevitability of the deconstruction of self that fallback invites us to allows us to come into contact with the divine in us, in others, in the world, in spirit. But not the divine as only light, but the divine as the truest marriage of light and shadow, of wholeness.

Nearly a decade ago, McCallum observed, "That kind of disorientation and sense of suffering from fallback will actually prompt a kind of reflection process. And if we actually do get to the point of revising our perspectives, our biases, then a kind of transformation has taken place that has widened our view. It's given us another level of depth in our interpersonal, social intelligence. And that becomes a huge asset for the future."[6]

Walking this path will require a new level of patience and compassion. We will need patience to sit in the not knowing as we endeavor to tend the soil of loss. We will need compassion for ourselves and others as we stumble through our endeavors to support the seed that attempts to grow as we come to know ourselves, each other, and the world anew.

Fallback composting is not about having the answers but being pushed to the edge of our capacity and forging ourselves into the uncertainty that we are asking others to forge into. Fallback composting at the collective level must begin with a willingness to tend the soil of our own individual decline.

It may just be that decline is the very thing that our development needs, not only individually, but also at the collective and systemic levels. Perhaps fallback invites us to face into the darkness, to touch intimately the icky spaces in self and society, in order for something better to grow. Our collective fallback and our willingness to come into relationship with it may offer *katabasis*—the descent toward healing—that is needed at this time.

> *"I've stopped trying to handle the darkness. I let the darkness handle me instead. Most of the time all it wants to do is hold me for a while—slow me down, keep me from running, cover me up long enough to remember that being in the dark doesn't mean there's something wrong with me. It means I'm alive, and this is part of the deal."*
>
> —Barbara Brown Taylor, author, Episcopal priest[7]

CHAPTER 19
CONCLUSION ILLUMINATING THE FULLNESS OF YOU

The way that many of us conceive of development and growth is that we move through a stage and leave it behind. We become bigger because we no longer have that which made us smaller. I don't believe that to be true.

We construct our self-concept over time. We layer the explanations we give ourselves and others about the experiences we have, and then move on with life, forgetting all the constructing and layering we've done. It starts to feel like we can't remember who the builder was, let alone decide whether any of it still serves or needs renovating. In short, we spend much of our lives telling ourselves stories about who we are, and how we became so.

When we tell ourselves the story that we are who we are because we are no longer what we were before, we deny a vital part of our existence, our becoming. We reject the parts of self that brought us to this place and an honest recognition of the many selves we have grown into and sometimes through along the way. And we don't acknowledge that those earlier parts of self are still with us, sometimes stealing the show when we refuse to acknowledge them.

While we believe the stories we tell ourselves to be based in fact, they are subjective, constructed, often self-serving, and even more frequently self-limiting. Not only do they not allow us to form a relationship with the beautiful, imperfect, complex person *we* are, they do not allow us to form meaningful, honest relationships with *others* who themselves are beautiful, imperfect, and complex. And until we know self (as fully as we are capable), we cannot know how to support others in their development as humans. We need to understand the ground on which we stand in order to understand what we are standing for.

Our fallback characters remind us of a time when we were not as capable as we believe ourselves now to be, and that doesn't feel good. But the fact that they keep knocking on the stage door is proof that they haven't gone anywhere, and that we haven't yet discovered what our journey through those earlier stages of development was trying to reveal.

Fallback allows us to recognize that we are not one consistent, enduring self. We have a full cast of characters, and we can come to know them. We can cultivate the capacity to detect when we are not showing up as our better selves by noticing when our storyline has been derailed. We can be honest with ourselves (even if we're not immediately honest with others) about what's going on by coming to understand the origin stories of our characters. Once we turn on the ghost light within self, as the spirits of our full ensemble come onto the stage to reveal themselves to us, we come to see the many scenes of our lives that they have been present in. We become aware of when the scene needs to be rewritten, when the set needs to be rearranged, or even when we need to ditch the script that has dictated our choices in order to set ourselves up for success. We are able to be intentional about who needs to be cast in the scenes of our lives, for what purpose. We can come to accept that we are the whole thing, the full company of bigness and smallness.

I'm cultivating a capacity to love the shadowy characters in myself. They are integral to my growing into the story of my life. Not the story that others have written for me or the one that plays without notice on repeat. My shadowy characters hold the key to my being able to write the script that allows me to live in alignment with my purpose and my values. They hold the key for you, too.

I get that it doesn't feel this way when they are setting the costumes on fire, commandeering the stage and stealing the show, or crumbling in shame and regret. But when we invite them into the soft glow of the ghost light, listen to the lines that they've been struggling their whole lives to read, and pay attention to the storyline they foreshadow, we're able to open up possibilities that allow them to use the full stage, to experiment with other ways of playing their roles that don't involve thrashing the set. When we leave the ghost light burning, we see that the torch these characters carry is meant to illuminate the whole of self, not to burn the whole thing down.

Fallback shines a spotlight on our darkest fears and our deepest yearnings; some that are available to us only when we are forced to sit in the more compressed space outside of the locked doors of our developmental house; some to which we have heretofore never been granted access. This illumination is not meant to make the darkness smaller. Instead, it offers us a lay of the journey, a journey toward becoming more fully and authentically human.

When we embrace our fallback, we come into a deeper knowing, a more honest truth. We realize that we do not always show up our best, most complex selves. We see that we are not consistent in our meaning-making, and we stop expecting to be. Understanding fallback allows us to find empathy for ourselves. We can begin to release the shame and self-judgment, and in so doing we are able to also relinquish our judgment of others. When we see that this, too, is me, we are able to take a broader perspective on other's experiences. Seeing and accepting ourselves in our smallness allows us to see others in their smallness, offer compassion, and accept and love them, too. If we are lucky, we might have someone who will offer the same to us.

When Diego sunk into the depths of his despair following his fallback with Kyra, she said to him, "I know you are in the depth of the pit. May I join you there with a candle, a blanket, and a ladder?"

May we all have someone who will join us in the darkness of fallback with a candle to serve as the ghost light on our stage, a blanket of love and acceptance, and a ladder to help us climb out of the orchestra pit when we have fallen back. It is my hope that this book has served in some small way this role for you.

AFTERWORD
STILL FENCING THE FIELD OF FALLBACK

In 2008, David McCallum observed the phenomenon of fallback in all eighteen of his research participants. His empirical documentation of fallback in individuals who had been assessed as making sense from stages all along the developmental spectrum provided a research-based understanding of the fallback phenomenon that had to that point only been theoretically speculated upon.[1]

Armed with the knowledge gained from McCallum's research and my own pilot study about the lived experience of fallback, in 2012 I set out to fence the theoretical field of fallback. I was accompanied in my discovery by six individuals, key thinkers in the fields of human and leadership development, three of whom were pioneers of adult development theory. Over the course of six months, I plumbed the depths of constructive developmental theory, situating the phenomenon of fallback within it in the company of Bill Torbert, Bob Kegan, Susanne Cook-Greuter, Jennifer Garvey Berger, Chuck Palus, and David McCallum. Ultimately, I came to a theory for understanding fallback informed by the wisdom and wonderings of these six thought leaders.[2]

Though there were pockets of agreement, to be sure, there was no set consensus about the distinctions of fallback amongst the key thinkers. It was my strenuous yet utterly joyful job to sift through all of the knowledge and speculations, unpacking the nuances of the theory and thoughtful exploration of the lived human experience, and come up with what I thought made most sense.

I mapped the terrain as best I could, given what was known and the sense I was able to make of it at the time, and I planted a stake in the ground:

> Fallback is the occurrence of individuals unintentionally making meaning from an earlier stage of development than is their center-of-gravity, meaning-making structure. During fallback, there is a temporary absence of all other options to think, feel, or behave differently.

Then I spent the next nine years testing this definition out as I explored the lived experience of fallback with hundreds of individuals in classrooms, in workplaces, in relationships, in life. And I had my theory for understanding fallback corrected in the process. I learned so much more about fallback in the years following my original research, knowledge that I've shared with the reader in the chapters of this book.

While it is so very important to claim what we do know, it is equally important to acknowledge those things that remain a mystery, that themselves need a ghost light shined on them. Fallback invites us to walk the talk of development both in our lived experience and in our naming with humility all that we still may not know.

So as I neared completion of this book, I invited the key thinkers to talk about fallback together for the first time. Throughout my original research, I'd had the incredible privilege of being in the company of these brilliant humans in one-on-one interviews, but we never were *all together* discussing what we were coming to know and theorize about.

On May 11, 2021, the key thinkers and I gathered together in what had become the pandemic-ubiquitous Zoom room to explore fallback, what we have noticed in the near decade since the original research, what we have been curious about, and the things that we still do not know. In this afterword, you will see that we are still fencing the field as we seek to illuminate the phenomenon of fallback.

Our conversation began with a good deal of surveying anew the territory we covered nearly a decade prior as we continued to refine the criteria and definition of fallback. The variables of choice, functionality, pleasure, the distance between stages, and the fleeting or enduring nature of fallback emerged as lingering curiosities about fallback.

Choice, Function, Pleasure

Bill Torbert observed, "One of the things that being aware of this fallback phenomenon from Val's and David's research has done for me, has changed about my interior life, is that I just notice much more frequently during the day which action logic I'm fundamentally performing from. And in many cases, I'm perfectly happy with it. The added dollop of awareness gives me a little bit of flexibility about not typing until my fingers and wrists are so sore that I literally can't bear it any longer, which is one of my Expert tendencies. But in the meantime, the creation of the bibliography, or whatever very Expert-ish kind of thing I'm doing, is enjoyable, and feels functional."

Chuck Palus remarked, "I resonate with that, Bill. Being in the Expert action logic is fun. It's effective. We know how to do it. And so, if it's enjoyable, is it fallback? It seems like the earlier action logics do have a lot of gifts to them. For me, there's a gift in being a good Diplomat. I'm really happy when I'm a good Diplomat or a good Expert. Achiever, less so—I'm less attracted to that one. But I do a lot of heavy lifting in my life in those places."[3]

However, Palus emphasized that though the gifts of the earlier stages were sometimes apparent, he wasn't convinced that he was always intentionally making the choice to access those action logics. Palus explained, "Part of the introspection I've been doing on this subject is about how much choice am I making in these moves. When I get pulled into the pleasure of being an Expert, I'm not sure I'm making that choice all the time. There's something in me that responds. As to whether I get in trouble or I get in happiness, it's not always choiceful. I slide into being a Diplomat, and then only later do I realize that maybe I had a choice, or that it was bad news that I slid into it or good news, but sometimes it is good news."

Palus speculated, "It's kind of a philosophical question, how much choice we really have. How much of this is the ego saying—because the ego is always prideful—'Well, yeah, I had a choice. I made a choice'? And how much of it just happens to us?" Palus pointed to the miniscule nature of the ego, the part of self that says "I am" held up against our tendency for the inflation of our self-regard. "Then we get into a little bit of the free will topic. We like to think we have free will in making these moves and choices. And as a humanist, I'm convinced we do, but not totally convinced, I guess."

The factors of choice and pleasure that were the focus of Torbert's and Palus's explorations were present in an example that Jennifer Garvey Berger shared with me nine years earlier. As she described a situation of falling back, she recalled, "I got angry, and I felt my perspective narrow, and I felt myself blaming another person. I knew that I was going to come to think that that was unfair. I knew that I was going to realize that I had been at fault, or at least partially at fault, that we had created this situation together. And I actually wanted to *not* have that bigger perspective in the moment."

Jennifer continued, "When you get angry, you get kind of a rush of I guess it's testosterone through your veins. I really wanted to prolong that feeling because I don't get it very often. And I actually tried to hold onto it for a couple of extra minutes. There was something powerful about it. There was something, not pleasurable, but full, alive, in it."

Berger described her experience of the moment of fallback. "I was hurt. And I knew that I had lost the ability to actually take another person's perspective. I was just locked down into my perspective. I knew that in that moment I didn't have my full capacities. I knew that I was not bringing my best biggest self. But I didn't have even the smallest doubt that I was going to be able to get it back. Still it feels like a loss. It feels like I can bend but look what I *can't* do. I know the things that I can do. I have a lot of theory around this, I have a lot of language, I have a whole lot of distinctions. I know that I can usually do these things. Look at me now. I *can't* do those things. I don't have them. In that moment I thought, *Wow! Look how little I am right now. Look at that.*"[4]

In the experience of fallback that Berger described, she was aware of herself shrinking, and she wanted to linger in that shrunken space. There was something about it that felt full and enlivening. Yet, despite her awareness of her smallness and even her desire to sink into the experience of it, she knew she was unable to bring her bigger self, the full suite of capacities she would normally have, to the moment. At the same time, she knew that this was a temporary experience; that what was lost in that moment of fallback would be found.

As we collectively wondered about the distinctions marking fallback, Berger summarized, "So there's functional and dysfunctional experiences of this thing. The experience of fallback that I described felt good, but it was not functional. There's choice and not choice. I don't think those are the same. I think you can be functional and not choiceful at the same time. And you can be choiceful and dysfunctional at the same time. So I think that those are different dynamics."

Torbert reminded us of situations in which there may be an intentional choice to operate from the perspective of the earlier meaning-making structure. He explained, "When one goes to a new job, it makes sense to start by making sure you get an adequate salary—Opportunist. Then it makes sense to learn the culture instead of being a smartass—Diplomat. And then it makes sense to be a smartass, because you've established yourself, and so forth. I mean those inner octaves, if we're hung up on any one of them, we have repeated chances to work on it in a way."

Without question, having a broader array of tools and options available to choice-fully deploy at key moments is one of the benefits of development. By virtue of having navigated and transitioned through these earlier stages oneself, one has acquired the gifts of their ways of being and knowing. Yet, if we are in fact "hung up on" any one of these earlier stages, though the acting from them may well be functional, may feel pleasurable, is it actually choiceful?

In the definition that I came to at the end of my research, fallback was unintentional. You were not making the choice to operate from an earlier stage of development. It just took you over, and you didn't have other options. It's fallback when the earlier form of mind chooses you, but not when you choose it. The question of who or what is doing the choosing becomes even murkier in the space between two contiguous stages.

Proximity

As we considered the features and subcategories of fallback and what counts and what may not, Torbert offered another parameter for consideration: the distance between one's center-of-gravity, meaning-making stage and the stage to which one has fallen back. Specifically, Torbert suggested that it's not fallback if the stage to which you have fallen is the immediate prior stage to your primary meaning-making capacity.

Torbert shared with the group, "One of the ways in which I disagree with the definition of fallback now, and maybe I did to begin with but didn't know it yet, is that people very often talk about acting from the immediate preceding stage to which their now center of gravity lies. And they call that fallback. And I think that's rarely the case. I mean, it's still part of their operative program. And I would expect to find it intermixed, often in an effective way, with the leading action logic. So I think it might be unusual for a one-stage-down action logic to be referred to as fallback."

I asked Torbert, "Are you pointing to developmental transition? That if a person is still in the process of transitioning from one stage to the next, when they dip into the earlier stage, it's not fallback? Or are you suggesting that it should rarely count as fallback if one has securely transitioned to a stage, but they are acting, thinking, feeling from the immediate prior stage?"

Torbert responded, "Certainly, if a person is scored as either late or early in transition between two action logics, I would not count action based in the earlier of the two action logics as fallback, unless further evidence from the action's structure and context persuasively suggests so." He elaborated, "I say action from the action logic prior to one's current center-of-gravity action logic is frequently *not* properly interpreted as fallback because, although one may measure as having the capacity for the current action logic, the process of weaving the new action logic thoroughly into one's day-to-day behavioral competences is a gradual one, entailing a continuing back-and-forth with the newly transcended action logic."[5]

One of the simplifications of stage development theory is that you make meaning, you behave, your entire form of mind is *in* one stage or another. When you brush the surface of the theories, you'll find handy, descriptive names of each of the developmental levels that seem to suggest that when you are in a stage, you have arrived solidly there. However, when you dig deeper into the theory, you find that there are many nuances in the space between each distinct developmental stage. In fact, in Kegan's developmental assessment,

The Subject/Object Interview, there are four measurable points in between two contiguous meaning-making systems.[6]

We don't make meaning from one stage of development until we suddenly awaken one morning solidly secure in the next. The meaning-making moves are nuanced and incremental. Much of the time, we float somewhere in the space in between stages rather than concretely rooted in a given action logic or order of mind.

Accordingly, the process of developmental transition is often more piecemeal than we generally paint it. It involves tremendous loss as the accoutrements of the stage that has held us so securely begin to grow tight and constricting. What made so much sense before no longer does. We have an innate understanding that this meaning-making structure no longer fits us, yet it is what we have known, and what comes next is uncertain. We move toward the next stage in our development in halting sprints, and sometimes crawls, and at times we race back into the arms of the stage that we have known, even though there's something not quite right about the goodness of fit. Developmental transition is marked by a seesaw motion between that which is known, which is coming to feel ever more constricting, and a new and unfamiliar costume that we are still growing into.

In the nine years post-original research, having heard many individuals claim fallback when he suspected they were merely in the process of developmental transition, Torbert wanted to make clear that it's not fallback if the earlier stage you are acting from is the one just prior to your center-of-gravity action logic.

In my original research on fallback, given the stochastic nature of developmental transition that Torbert articulated, several of the key thinkers also made the distinction between fallback and the normal back-and-forth movement that occurs during developmental transition. Yet, McCallum and Palus were on the fence about whether developmental transition, the last hurrah in a given stage, should be considered fallback. They noted at the time that if being more explicit about the likelihood of falling back during developmental transition might help people understand what is happening, accept it, lean into it, and have hope, yielding a better outcome, then maybe there is merit to doing so.[7]

Separately, there are the times that Torbert also referenced when the structure and context suggest that the individual is indeed firmly rooted in the next later stage for which fallback could truly be considered fallback, not developmental transition. When this is the case, it seems arbitrary to exclude exploration based solely on proximity of the fallen-back-to stage to the one from which one has fallen back. The stage immediately prior can still provide just as deep and dark a hole for one to slip unconsciously into as one of our earlier, more primitive stages.

Transitory vs. Enduring: Living in the Range or Tethered Deeply

The commonplace nature of fallback and the apparent strength and depth of the tether to an earlier developmental space emerged as another distinguishing factor in fallback. Palus offered to the group an observation he's been making since he and I began exploring fallback together nearly a decade ago. We tend to pose fallback as something that rarely happens. Yet fallback would seem to be the norm of daily life.

Palus noted, "The temporary version of fallback seems very common, such that it's almost the rule rather than the exception. It seems to me that every day I experience fallback if it means unintentionally slipping into something more primitive. And David, in your research, I noticed every one of your eighteen cases expressed fallback. I guess that's one of the issues I have with it. If it's sort of the norm, we seem to be treating it as an anomaly."

Berger agreed, "Chuck, I hear your question. If we are all so commonly doing this, then is it a *this* that we're doing? Or is it just living in some way? And so, I wonder how we make that distinction. I have this idea that there's our ordinary self, and then we sometimes reach into a bigger self when we're around those people or contexts that augment us. But we can live kind of fluidly in there. And then sometimes we visit this smaller self, because of the context, or the mood, or whatever—what we had for breakfast or didn't. But we kind of live in those. That's what I think of Susanne Cook-Greuter's and Bill's idea of a range, from that bigger self all the way to that smaller self."

"So how much do we need to deviate from those places before we get into something that you would call unusual, or you would give a different label to fallback?" Berger asked. "How much variation would we think of as just *Tuesday*? It's just what life is. And there are a really interesting set of questions there."

Palus offered, "There are also Ken Wilber's lines of development to consider." Wilber's theory posits that we not only have stages of development, but there also exist lines of development that are at various points of maturation (e.g., the musical line, the spiritual line, the somatic line, etc.).[8] In other words, we may be more highly developed in one line, such as our spiritual line than we are in another, such as our musical line. Palus continued, "Maybe each of us has these lines. We can't even discern them. They're not always nameable. But we could find ourselves all of a sudden slipping into a realm in which we're just not as developed there. Is that fallback? Or is that just stepping into a place that's not as developed?"

McCallum shared his own example of fallback that also pointed to an aspect of self that was not developed. McCallum, a Jesuit priest, recently took a post at the Vatican in Rome, relocating from his home state of New York. He shared, "This transition to Rome has been so hard. Learning Italian has been so hard. Working to function in a medieval culture has been so hard. And I'm finding myself needing to go back to all kinds of earlier parts of myself that just weren't well-integrated so that I have them as resources right now. And I realize much of that is related to interactions with parents and others when I was a child and wanting to be the good boy. And so, this way in which fallback can sometimes put us right back to a somewhat habitual or patterned earlier self that we have available to us, in a sense, to reintegrate, I think is an opportunity and a challenge."

In contrast to being a part of self that wasn't developed because it didn't need to be, as sometimes happens with our lines of development, this aspect of McCallum's development seems to have been one that got stuck in an earlier developmental space *in spite of* being necessary. What McCallum described points to a falling back to an earlier self, accompanied by an invitation to integrate it from the level of complexity to which he now has access.

McCallum remarked, "There's also the issue of what happens in conditions of trauma provoking fallback to these earlier selves, where people, in a sense, sectioned off, unconsciously, parts of their personalities as defensive moves to survive at that moment, and the story and the process of reintegrating those. There's such a spectrum of how trauma shows up in people's lives. And I think what we're discovering is that more and more of us have had some minor or major traumas that have affected us, foreshortening the development that would have happened had the trauma not interrupted. The degree to which these encapsulated selves continue to exist as sub-personalities or as parts of our unconscious, I just find very interesting as a dimension of how we think about fallback and also the process of integration."

Some of our experiences of fallback are transitory, only momentary, dissipating as quickly as they arise. Some experiences of fallback are more enduring, pointing to encapsulated parts of self. These bracketed off parts of self, such as the one McCallum described with his move to Rome, occurred around aspects of self that were in need of developing, that still need tending to, that continue to present themselves throughout our lives. Some of these encapsulations were formed through trauma at an earlier place in our development.

Indeed, whether our experiences of fallback seem to be those precipitated by life on a Tuesday or are anchored to a part of self that was left behind in our development, the gift of fallback may only be discovered as we shift our relationship to it, to us in our smallness. As we explored what does and does not mark the experience of fallback, I began to wonder if the distinctions around the duration of the fallback or the rooted-in-ness of the tether suggest that each type of fallback should be treated differently. Would one type of fallback be less illustrative or revealing in our coming to know and accept the full terrain of self? And might our experiences of fallback, passing or elongated as they may be, allow us to apply our learning across context?

As-Yet Integrated vs. New Context for which There Has Been No Opportunity to Integrate

Nine years ago, Palus offered an alternative framing for fallback. He referenced child development pioneer Jean Piaget's concept of *decalage*. Decalage refers to the differing ability over time and with practice for one to adeptly apply a new learning from one context to a different context. It suggests that development, the capacities that we are able to bring to the table from one context to the next, is fragmented.

Palus wondered if another category of fallback should be created called *pseudo fallback* or *apparent fallback* that names those learning experiences that have similar characteristics to fallback but may just be about new learning or even old learning now being practiced and mastered in a new context.[9]

I had forgotten about Palus's references to learning being applied in a different context as an alternative framing for fallback. Then my colleague Halim Dunsky, having read an early draft of this section, referenced Piaget's decalage. Dunsky's reference to Piaget brought me back to Palus's wonderings from a decade prior.

Dunsky remarked, "So many new variables are contributing to the current context—global warming, Covid, the assault on democracy, etc. In your exploration of fallback, there's an expressed sense that these conditions draw people back from competencies that have been previously demonstrated and stabilized in other contexts. Yet how can we claim to be able to detect a retrenchment from some established stable capacity *in that context which we have never seen before?*"

Dunsky explained, "We go home to our family of origin for the holidays, and it feels like we revert to the teenager we used to be. We are suddenly embedded in, subject to, the kind of psychodynamics that we sail past in our more evolved state in our usual life. But have we really lost those skills when we face our mother? Or might it be more accurate to say they were never achieved in the mother context in the first place? The fallback concept points to some kind of generalized ability that disappears, but can we distinguish that from simply a combination of circumstances for which the ability never developed? So the stressors actually could be said to be showing unintegrated territory, a growth opportunity, rather than causing a regress."[10]

Dunsky was now, as Palus had earlier been, wondering if what is often described as fallback is actually a falling back to an earlier space that was known or rather an encountering of new territory to which a capacity from another aspect of one's knowing may be brought to bear. In other words, it is not so much a falling back as an expansion of the application of meaning- making to a new context.

Our yearning to clean up the model of human development, to make it presentable and clear and distinguishable to others, may lead us to want to articulate the distinctions and subcategories that are the focus of this afterword. We want to know what counts and what doesn't so we can draw the lines around this phenomenon of fallback clearly for others. The distinctions—intentional/unintentional, functional/dysfunctional, pleasure/pain, the distance between stages, the regularity and strength of the pull to fallback, or falling back to a place we have known or an invitation to knew learning—are helpful as we continue to map the territory of fallback, to determine where it fits in the theory. Yet, in practice, in the real-life seeking to know the fullness of one's self, the purpose of exploring the terrain may be different. Just as we humans are exquisitely complicated, so too is the theory of human development. And fallback, well, it muddies up the theory even further. And that's not a bad thing.

GRATEFUL FORS

(as my family refers to them...traditionally known as **Acknowledgements***)*

Sometimes we don't know a thing to be a possibility until someone puts the idea right in front of us. Such was the case with this book. Bill Torbert was the first to declare that I would write a book about fallback as if it was a fait accompli. Though I had not before even given it a thought, once Bill said it, I knew it to be true. Bill, I'm grateful for your planting the seed those many years ago from which this book would grow; for planting the many seeds of connection in the field of adult development that would serve as fertilizer to my emerging knowing and becoming in this space.

Bill Torbert was one of six who accompanied me in my seminal research situating the phenomenon of fallback in constructive developmental theory. I'm grateful for each of these "key thinkers." David McCallum for going first—identifying the phenomenon of fallback in individuals at places all along the developmental spectrum in his research and providing the launch pad from which my own research would take flight. Bill Torbert, Susanne Cook-Greuter, and Bob Kegan for their humility in allowing me to probe the theories that they had helped develop and their generosity of thought and curiosity as we wondered together what else may be true. Jennifer Garvey Berger for her elegant interweaving and elucidation of the fields of leadership and adult development and her love for the humans at the core of each. Chuck Palus for his awesome capacity to gently question and wonder about a theory in order to hold all of its truths and for inspiring me to do the same. The experience of articulating the phenomenon of fallback with each of these key thinkers a decade ago has been one of the gifts of my career—a gift that I had the joy of encountering again and again throughout the research and writing of this book.

Fred Jones sparked the idea to use theater as a metaphor to access and explore our experiences of fallback. The idea was further kindled through our collaboration with Michael Berger through which Fred's powerful tool, *Emergent Play*, was honed. *Emergent Play* formed the basis for the research protocol and practice components that are featured in the *Your Turn* sections throughout the book. I'm forever grateful for Fred's tool-building genius, his regular "rooting for you" emails that somehow always arrived at the precise moment I needed the encouragement, and his generosity in allowing me to build upon his ideas and good questions in service to a more authentic relationship with our full ensemble of self.

While Fred inspired the idea of using the metaphor of theater as a way to come to know our full cast of characters, it was the artist Rachel Phillips who brought the imagery of the ghost light into luminous and evocative focus through her "Ghost Light Theaters" which served as a visual muse to my writing. I'm grateful for Rachel's artistic genius and her generosity in allowing me to adorn the cover of this book with her "Backstage" theater and an image from her "Sculpture" montage. The full series of theaters and montages can be found at www.TreadwellPress.com. I'm smitten with them all.

Diego, Robbin, and Octavia—you are the stars of this book. I'm grateful for your courage in stepping into the ghost light and inviting your characters onto the stage, listening to the lines they'd been waiting their whole lives to read, and welcoming the lessons that they were there to teach you—and allowing me, and now the reader, to serve as the audience to the evolving play of your development. I learned so much from you about fallback, about vulnerability, about being human. It has been my great privilege to accompany you in your evolving relationship with your fallback, with your full ensemble of self, these many years.

To the countless individuals whose stories are not explicitly told in this book but who have invited me to walk beside you in your own illumination, I'm grateful for your allowing me to sit at your feet, witness, and learn.

There are so many others without whose wisdom, thought partnership, encouragement, mad wordsmithing skills, and generosity this book would not have come into being...or at least its *beingness* would have been greatly diminished.

Cheryl Getz, Terri Monroe, and Lea Hubbard tended the seedling of my emerging academic and full human self at the University of San Diego. From these three I learned how to be in inquiry about not only what is "out there" but also "in here," and how to use the discoveries of both to inform a deeper knowing.

In writing, for me, getting started is the hardest part. Chuck Palus, Zafer Achi, Bill Torbert, Jennifer Garvey Berger, Karen Horning, Cara Taylor Miller, and Aliki Nicolaides—your thoughtful and pointed suggestions, critiques, and praise on the early drafts of this book were integral to my being able to figure out what it was that I needed to say and organizing it in a way that it could best be received.

Gideon Culman's invitation to speak about fallback at the beginning of the Covid-19 lockdown brought me out of my head and my computer where the ideas and stories in this book had been percolating, and onto the "stage" of his podcasts where they could be of use to people on a broader scale.

David McCallum's suggestion that I write an article on fallback in pandemic times, and the brainstorming that ensued, sparked a reframing of the steps involved in our coming into relationship with our fallback that informed the way I write about fallback in this book.

Elise Foster, Gideon Culman, Dee Scull, Tom Draffen, and Staffan Åkerblom—your thought-partnership and our collaborations helped shape the invitations to the Ghost Light programs while concurrently shaping the exercises that I invite the reader into throughout the book. I'm grateful for you and so many others including Hilary Bradbury, Bill Torbert, and Julia Kukard who were determined that an understanding of fallback make it out into the world so it can do good and for providing the platform to make it so.

To all of those who have patiently and persistently accompanied me through the years of this book's writing, with its attendant flurries of activity and periodic lulls, thank you for your regular check-ins, your excitement for whatever stage I happened to be in, your patience through the times of inactivity, your reminders that this work is important, and your excitement to share it with others. Shakiyla Smith, Aliki Nicolaides, Toni Rushing, Dana Carman, Tom Cesarini,

Justine Kozo, Lori Geist, Olga Cohoon—your encouragement and companionship in its many forms sustained me.

I'm grateful for my editor, Erica Ellis, who graciously navigated both my shifting schedule and my ever-growing word count. Your on-point feedback about what aspects of lived experience and theory should be revealed, how, and at what point made the storytelling stronger, clearer, and more connected.

Jennifer Garvey Berger and Brian Emerson made the process of publishing this book feel less daunting through their generosity of time, connections, and wisdom borne of their own experiences.

So many of the names listed above belong to people who I have come to know and love through the communities that I have had the privilege to be a part for more than a decade. The relationships I've formed with those at the University of San Diego, in the Growth Edge Network, and in the Action Inquiry Community have been sources of meaningful collaborations and even more profound friendships. In these spaces I have played and experimented and had my ideas prodded and honed as I was pushed to the edge of my own knowing. All the while I felt beautifully and securely held in my discovery. I'm grateful to all who comprise these communities for the good questions and the good company.

My deepest gratitude goes to my family.

I offer my unending love and appreciation to my sister, Stephanie Townsend, who had a front row seat as the origin stories of my life were written, who both witnessed and triggered so many of my fallback characters, and who also called forth my characters of grace...and loved and accepted them all. That I could bring all of me to you in both the triumphs and the agonies of writing this book (and of life) filled my soul and bolstered my capacity to stretch into the uncomfortable places within and outside of me. Jeannie Conrad, I'm grateful to you for stepping in to fill this role when Stephanie could no longer. Her voice, her presence, her wisdom, and her love flow through you.

Sonnie Livesay, thank you for settling in for the long ride of this book-birthing and story-unfolding with me. Thank you for allowing me to reveal you as I illuminated me. Thank you for knowing, and seeing, and loving the fullness of me.

Townsend and Sloane Livesay—you are my most profound purpose, my most impactful teachers, my greatest source of inspiration. Thank you for providing the mirror through which I could see myself more honestly, for revealing the storylines that no longer serve, and for your patience as I learn the ropes of the most important role I'll ever have.

Lastly, to those who have had the courage to step into the ghost light and for those who will, I am grateful for you.

NOTES

Introduction
1. Sense-making and meaning-making will be used throughout this book. Both describe how we understand and assign meaning to our experiences.

Chapter 1 – The Fluidity of Development
1. Valerie T. Livesay, "Exploring the Paradoxical Role and Experience of Fallback in Developmental Theory," PhD diss., (University of San Diego, 2013).
2. William R. Torbert, *Action Inquiry: The Secret of Timely and Transforming Leadership* (San Francisco, CA: Berrett-Koehler Publishers, Inc., 2004).
3. David C. McCallum, Jr., "Exploring the Implications of a Hidden Diversity in Group Relations Conference Learning: A Developmental Perspective," EdD diss., (Columbia University, 2008).
4. McCallum. "Exploring Implications of Hidden Diversity."
5. In May 2021, the key thinkers and I gathered together to talk about fallback collectively for the first time. During this conversation, we explored what we don't know, what we are curious about, and what an understanding of fallback may offer us as we make our way into a post- and enduring- pan-pandemic world. Hereafter, references to this conversation will be noted as "Fallback Key Thinker Reconvening, May 2021."
6. Torbert, *Action Inquiry*. Torbert's theory of adult development consists of seven primary developmental action logics. Those in the Transforming action logic generate organizational and personal transformations. (See Chapter 8 endnotes for more detail.)

7. Elaine Herdman-Barker and Nancy C. Wallis, "Imperfect Beauty: Hierarchy and Fluidity in Leadership Development," *Challenging Organisations and Society* 5 (May 2016): 879.
8. Fallback Key Thinker Reconvening, May 2021.
9. Herdman-Barker and Wallis, "Imperfect Beauty," 879
10. Herdman-Barker and Wallis, "Imperfect Beauty," 866
11. Herdman-Barker and Wallis, "Imperfect Beauty," 867.

Chapter 2 – What is Fallback?
1. Livesay, "Exploring Fallback."

Chapter 4 – Ghost Light
1. The idea to use theater as a metaphor to explore people's experiences of fallback was sparked during a collaboration with Fred Jones. Fred, using his mad skills and creativity, built on a framework called the Stage Page, which was developed by Barbara Lanebrown to develop a tool called "Emergent Play." I had the good fortune to hang around Fred and try out the early versions of the tool, offering my opinion and wondering aloud about how this theater analogy might help us better understand and explore the multiplicity of characters that make us up and how coming to know these might help us better connect to and claim our experiences of fallback. The theater-oriented framework that I use in my research and practice has been powerfully influenced by Fred's tool-building genius.

Chapter 5 – Noticing
1. Valerie Livesay, interview with Gideon Culman, *Pandemic Companions*, podcast audio, March 19, 2020, http://pandemiccompanions.libsyn.com/falling-back.
2. McCallum, "Exploring Implications of Hidden Diversity."
3. Livesay, "Exploring Fallback."
4. Livesay, "Exploring Fallback."
5. Livesay, "Exploring Fallback."
6. Livesay, "Exploring Fallback."
7. Livesay, "Exploring Fallback."
8. Robert Kegan, *The Evolving Self: Problem and Process in Human Development* (Cambridge: Harvard University Press, 1982). In Kegan's theory, what is subject is part of who one is and what is object is separate from who one is. What is subject does not exist outside of us. It is an integrated aspect of one's self. It is one's subjectivity. As what is

subject moves over to what is object in the process of developmental movement, it becomes distinct, different, capable of being reflected upon objectively. A more robust description of the subject/object transition can be found in chapter 8, Reflecting.
9. Fallback Key Thinker Reconvening, May 2021.

Chapter 8 – Reflecting
1. Kegan, *Evolving Self*.
2. Torbert, *Action Inquiry*. Torbert defines action logic as an overall strategy that so thoroughly informs our experience that we cannot see it. Action logics reflect the dynamic, multiple dimensions of a person's experience, including reasoning and behavior. Torbert's theory of adult development consists of seven primary developmental action logics: Opportunist – Wins for self in any way possible; Diplomat – Wants to belong and fit in; Expert – Focuses on logic and expertise; Achiever – Driven by personal and team achievement; Redefining – Reframes complex problems in unique ways; Transforming – Generates organizational and personal transformations; Alchemical – Integrates material, spiritual, and societal transformations.
3. Livesay, "Exploring Fallback."
4. Fallback Key Thinker Reconvening, May 2021.
5. Donald A. Schoen, *The Reflective Practitioner: How Professionals Think in Action* (New York: Basic Books, 1983).
6. This piece of wisdom didn't make it into my dissertation, but it was generated through my research for it with Jennifer Garvey Berger (Livesay, "Exploring Fallback.")
7. Schoen, *Reflective Practitioner*.
8. Torbert, *Action Inquiry*. What is described throughout this section is the practice that Torbert refers to as *action inquiry*. "Action inquiry is a way of simultaneously conducting action and inquiry as a disciplined leadership practice that increases the wider effectiveness of our actions" (p. 1) …and… "interweaves research and practice in the present." (p. 6)
9. David Rock and Jeffrey Schwartz, "Reclaiming Children and Youth: The Journal of Strength-Based Interventions," *The Neuroscience of Leadership* 16, no. 3 (2007): 15
10. Rock and Schwartz, "Reclaiming Children" in Livesay, "Exploring Fallback," 64-65.

Chapter 11 – Recognizing Triggers
1. David Rock, "SCARF: A Brain-Based Model for Collaborating with and Influencing Others," *NeuroLeadership Journal* 1 (2008).
2. Rock, "SCARF."
3. Rock and Schwartz, "Reclaiming Children."; Rock, "SCARF."
4. Livesay, "Exploring Fallback."; Valerie T. Livesay, "One Step Back, Two Steps Forward: Fallback in Human and Leadership Development," *Journal of Leadership, Accountability and Ethics* 12, no. 4 (2015): 173-189. Originally, physiological brain responses were included as one of the overarching triggers I identified in my research. However, over the years I've come to realize that rather than serving as a trigger in their own right, physiological brain responses are activated as a result of the other triggers that hijack the prefrontal cortex where higher order meaning-making takes place and relegate our sense-making to the amygdala—the territory of fight, flight, or freeze
5. Valerie Livesay, "From Fallback to Spring Forward: Bringing our Better Selves in Times of Complexity," *Medium,* April 13, 2020, https://medium.com/@vlivesay/from-fallback-to-spring-forward-bringing-our-better-selves-in-times-of-complexity-ccf5a3508f72?sk=d2def7bc162efaa9c190c72bc68d23c0.
6. Livesay, "Exploring Fallback."; Livesay, "Fallback to Spring Forward."
7. Jack Mezirow, "Understanding Transformation Theory," *Adult Education* Quarterly 44, no. 4 (1994): 222-232.
8. Livesay, "Exploring Fallback."; Livesay, "Fallback to Spring Forward."
9. Livesay, "Exploring Fallback."; Livesay, "Fallback to Spring Forward."
10. Livesay, "Exploring Fallback."; Livesay, "Fallback to Spring Forward."

Chapter 12 - Robbin – Recognizing Triggers
1. Livesay, "Exploring Fallback," 184-185.

Chapter 13 – Your Turn to Recognize Triggers
1. This exercise was adapted from Sophie Sabbage, *The Cancer Whisperer* (New York: Plume, 2017). Many of Sophie's tools are based on the work of Dr. K. Bradford Brown and his educational program originally called The Life Training, now called More To Life, with Dr. Roy Whitten.

Chapter 14 – Recovering & Growing
1. Fallback Key Thinker Reconvening, May 2021.
2. Livesay, "Exploring Fallback."; Livesay, "Fallback to Spring Forward."

3. Chris Argyris, Robert Putnam, and Diana Smith, *Action Science* (San Francisco: Jossey-Bass, 1985).
4. Livesay, "Exploring Fallback."; Livesay, "Fallback to Spring Forward."
5. Livesay, "Exploring Fallback," 142.
6. Livesay, "Exploring Fallback," 196.
7. Livesay, "Exploring Fallback," 195.; Livesay, "Fallback to Spring Forward," 184
8. Fallback Key Thinker Reconvening, May 2021.
9. In a recent online forum conversation, my colleague Dimitri Glazkov posed, "I wonder if fallback is developmental in itself. Recent fallback experiences seem to point at this idea that suddenly missing 'a room in the house' is a stepping-stone toward deeper reflection." Dimitri's wondering led to a rich exchange with our fellow colleagues Naryan Wong, Thomas Arta, and Daniel Kaufman exploring how one's mindset about fallback may determine whether it leads to what Glazkov coined a "virtuous or vicious cycle." Wong asked, "If one believes that fallback often precedes development, would that start a self-fulfilling process? If one views fallback as weakness, might they start to avoid difficult situations that may precede both growth and fallback?" Indeed, fallback has the capacity to lead to a virtuous cycle of growth, but it may also result in a vicious cycle of decline. Which way it goes may be closely correlated with one's developmental stage and one's narrative about and relationship to fallback. Dimitri Glazkov, Naryan Wong, Thomas Arta, Daniel Kaufman, Valerie Livesay, personal conversation, Growth Edge Network Slack Channel, May, 2021.
10. Livesay, "Exploring Fallback," 256-257.; Livesay, "Fallback to Spring Forward," 185.
11. Fallback Key Thinker Reconvening, May 2021.
12. David McCallum coined this gem, "Fallback is the window to our blind spots" at Fallback Key Thinker Reconvening, May 2021.
13. Livesay, "Exploring Fallback," 261.

Chapter 17 – Epilogue
1. The Self-Sovereign form of mind refers to Kegan's developmental stage in which an individual is not aware of their own impulses and wishes. They just are. Individuals in this form of mind can consider another's view, but only from the standpoint of how it impacts their own needs and wishes. Those operating from the Socialized form of

mind are able to reflect on their own wishes and impulses but are unable to see how they are influenced by others. Individuals making meaning from the Socialized form of mind internalize the beliefs, values, impressions, opinions, and feelings of others, and are not able to self-construct these. The Self-Authored form of mind is marked by perfectionism, certainty, self-maintenance and control, and independent accomplishment. Individuals in this order value personal autonomy and self-authorship. See Robert Kegan, *The Evolving Self: Problem and process in human development* (Cambridge: Harvard University Press, 1982). For an incredibly approachable understanding of Kegan's forms of mind, see Jennifer Garvey Berger, "Appendix A: Key concepts in adult development," *in Changing on the Job: Developing leaders for a complex world* (Stanford: Stanford University Press, 2012).
2. Torbert, *Action Inquiry.*

Chapter 18 – Leaving the Ghost Light Burning for Others
1. Fallback Key Thinker Reconvening, May 2021.
2. Spring Cheng, "The Return to the Earth Mother: An East-West Reckoning of Adult Development," *Resonance Path Institute* (blog), February 24, 2021, https://resonancepath.com/the-return-to-the-earth-mother/
3. Livesay, "Exploring Fallback."; Livesay, "Fallback to Spring Forward."
4. Livesay, "Exploring Fallback."; Livesay, "Fallback to Spring Forward."
5. Sabbage, *Cancer Whisperer,* 474, Kindle edition.
6. Livesay, "Exploring Fallback," 141-142.
7. Barbara Brown Taylor, "How We Survive Winter," *The New York Times,* December 20, 2020, https://www.nytimes.com/interactive/2020/12/20/us/how-to-survive-winter.html.

Afterword – Still Fencing the Field of Fallback
1. McCallum, "Exploring Implications of Hidden Diversity."
2. Livesay, "Exploring Fallback."
3. Torbert, *Action Inquiry.* As a reminder, Torbert defines action logic as an overall strategy that so thoroughly informs our experience that we cannot see it. Action logics reflect the dynamic, multiple dimensions of a person's experience, including reasoning and behavior. Torbert's theory of adult development consists of seven primary developmental action logics: *Opportunist* – Wins for self in any way possible; *Diplomat* – Wants to belong and fit in; *Expert* – Focuses on logic and expertise;

Achiever – Driven by personal and team achievement; *Redefining* – Reframes complex problems in unique ways; *Transforming* – Generates organizational and personal transformations; *Alchemical* – Integrates material, spiritual, and societal transformations.

4. Jennifer Garvey Berger, interview by Valerie T. Livesay, October 23, 2012, for dissertation research.
5. William R. Torbert, email communication with Valerie T. Livesay, June 15 to July 1, 2021.
6. Lisa Lahey, Emily Souvaine, Robert Kegan, Robert Goodman, Sally Felix, *A Guide to the Subject-Object Interview: Its Administration and Interpretation* (South Carolina: CreateSpace Independent Publishing Platform, 2011).
7. Livesay, "Exploring Fallback."
8. Ken Wilber, *Integral Psychology* (Boston: Shambhala, 2000). Many of us have experienced this underdevelopment of a line when we learned a particular subject in school only to the point that we were able to pass the test but had no further necessity to make use of this learning again, and certainly no ability to apply it beyond rote recitation.
9. Livesay, "Exploring Fallback."
10. Halim Dunsky, email communication with Valerie T. Livesay, November 1, 2021.

SELECTED BIBLIOGRAPHY

Argyris, Chris, Robert Putnam, and Diana Smith. *Action Science*. San Francisco: Jossey-Bass, 1985.

Berger, Jennifer Garvey. *Changing on the Job: Developing leaders for a complex world*. Stanford: Stanford University Press, 2012.

Cheng, Spring. "The Return to the Earth Mother: An east-west reckoning of adult development." *Resonance Path Institute* (blog), February 24, 2021. https://resonancepath.com/the-return-to-the-earth-mother/.

Herdman-Barker, Elaine and Nancy C. Wallis. "Imperfect Beauty: Hierarchy and Fluidity in Leadership Development." *Challenging Organisations and Society* 5 (May 2016): 866-885.

Kegan, Robert. *The Evolving Self: Problem and Process in Human Development*. Cambridge: Harvard University Press, 1982.

Lahey, Lisa, Emily Souvaine, Robert Kegan, Robert Goodman, and Sally Felix. *A Guide to the Subject-Object Interview: Its Administration and Interpretation*. South Carolina: CreateSpace Independent Publishing Platform, 2011.

Livesay, Valerie T. "Exploring the Paradoxical Role and Experience of Fallback in Developmental Theory." PhD diss. University of San Diego, 2013.

Livesay, Valerie T. "One Step Back, Two Steps Forward: Fallback in Human and Leadership Development." *Journal of Leadership, Accountability and Ethics* 12, no. 4 (October 2015): 173-189.

Livesay, Valerie. ("Falling Back.") Interview with Gideon Culman. *Pandemic Companions*. Podcast audio. March 19, 2020. http://pandemiccompanions.libsyn.com/falling-back.

Livesay, Valerie. "From Fallback to Spring Forward: Bringing Our Better Selves in Times of Complexity." *Medium*, April 13, 2020. https://medium.com/@vlivesay/from-fallback-to-spring-forward-bringing-our-better-selves-in-times-of-complexity-ccf5a3508f72?sk=d2def7bc162efaa9c190c72bc68d23c0

McCallum, Jr., David C. "Exploring the Implications of a Hidden Diversity in Group Relations Conference Learning: A Developmental Perspective." EdD diss. Columbia University, 2008.

Mezirow, Jack. "Understanding Transformation Theory." *Adult Education Quarterly* 44, no. 4 (1994): 222-232.

Rock, David and Jeffrey Schwartz. "Reclaiming Children and Youth: The Journal of Strength-based Interventions." *The Neuroscience of Leadership*, 16, no. 3 (2007).

Rock, David. "SCARF: A Brain-Based Model for Collaborating with and Influencing Others." *NeuroLeadership Journal*, 1 (2008).

Sabbage, Sophie. *The Cancer Whisperer*. New York: Plume, 2017.

Schoen, Donald A. *The Reflective Practitioner: How Professionals Think in Action*. New York: Basic Books, 1983.

Taylor, Barbara Brown. "How We Survive Winter." *The New York Times*, December 20, 2020, https://www.nytimes.com/interactive/2020/12/20/us/how-to-survive-winter.html.

Torbert, William R. *Action Inquiry: The Secret of Timely and Transforming Leadership*. San Francisco, CA: Berrett-Koehler Publishers, Inc., 2004.

Wilber, Ken. *Integral Psychology*. Boston: Shambhala, 2000.

ABOUT THE AUTHOR

For more than a decade, Valerie Livesay, PhD has been thinking about and inquiring into the phenomenon of fallback — when despite our optimal developmental capacities, what we often refer to as our developmental center-of-gravity, we make meaning, feel, and act from a smaller, less complex, less capable form of mind. Following a career in higher education in both administration and faculty roles, Valerie's present endeavors seek to extend the concepts and experiences that she studies, teaches, and writes about outside of the halls of academia, to the lives of all people trying to navigate the tricky business of showing up in alignment with their intentions in the many contexts of their world.

As Chief Illuminator at Ghost Light Leadership, Valerie accompanies individuals through their discovery of self using the analogy of theater to set the stage for their historical and unfolding story. She serves as documentarian, bringing to light the lesser known, lesser loved, and occasionally forgotten roles and scenes that make up one's full ensemble and storyline. Through her writing, speaking, coaching, and workshop offerings, Valerie invites the many characters that comprise the full ensemble of one's self to dance together in order to better meet their intentions.

Valerie lives in San Diego, California with her two cats, husband, and two children, with the latter three serving simultaneously as the most frequent protagonists of and audience to her experiences of fallback and the greatest source of her desire to do better.

To learn more, visit www.ghostlightleadership.com.

Printed in Great Britain
by Amazon